IMMERSION
Bible Studies

ISAIAH
JEREMIAH
LAMENTATIONS

Praise for IMMERSION

"IMMERSION BIBLE STUDIES is a powerful tool in helping readers to hear God speak through Scripture and to experience a deeper faith as a result."
Adam Hamilton, author of *24 Hours That Changed the World*

"If you're looking for a deeper knowledge and understanding of God's Word, you must dive into IMMERSION BIBLE STUDIES. Whether in a group setting or as an individual, you will experience God and his unconditional love for each of us in a whole new way."
Pete Wilson, founding and senior pastor of Cross Point Church

"This beautiful series helps readers become fluent in the words and thoughts of God, for purposes of illumination, strength building, and developing a closer walk with the One who loves us so."
Laurie Beth Jones, author of *Jesus, CEO* and *The Path*

"The IMMERSION BIBLE STUDIES series is no less than a game changer. It ignites the purpose and power of Scripture by showing us how to do more than just know God or love God; it gives us the tools to love like God as well."
Shane Stanford, author of *You Can't Do Everything . . . So Do Something*

"I highly commend to you IMMERSION BIBLE STUDIES, which tells us what the Bible teaches and how to apply it personally."
John Ed Mathison, author of *Treasures of the Transformed Life*

IMMERSION
Bible Studies

ISAIAH
JEREMIAH
LAMENTATIONS

Janice E. Catron

Abingdon Press

Nashville

ISAIAH, JEREMIAH, LAMENTATIONS
IMMERSION BIBLE STUDIES
by Janice E. Catron

Copyright © 2012 by Abingdon Press

Library of Congress Cataloging-in-Publication Data

Catron, Janice, 1955-
   Isaiah, Jeremiah, Lamentations / Janice E. Catron.
      p. cm. — (Immersion Bible studies)
   ISBN 978-1-4267-1637-9 (curriculum—printed text plus-cover : alk. paper) 1. Bible. O.T. Isaiah—Textbooks. 2. Bible. O.T. Jeremiah--Textbooks. 3. Bible. O.T. Lamentations—Textbooks. I. Title.
   BS1515.55.C38 2012
   224'.106—dc23

                                                            2012034851

Editor: Pamela Dilmore
Leader Guide Writer: Pamela Dilmore

12 13 14 15 16 17 18 19 20 21—10 9 8 7 6 5 4 3 2 1

Manufactured in the United States of America

Contents

Review Team

Diane Blum
Pastor
East End United Methodist Church
Nashville, Tennessee

Susan Cox
Pastor
McMurry United Methodist Church
Claycomo, Missouri

Margaret Ann Crain
Professor of Christian Education
Garrett-Evangelical Theological Seminary
Evanston, Illinois

Nan Duerling
Curriculum Writer and Editor
Cambridge, Maryland

Paul Escamilla
Pastor and Writer
St. John's United Methodist Church
Austin, Texas

James Hawkins
Pastor and Writer
Smyrna, Delaware

Andrew Johnson
Professor of New Testament
Nazarene Theological Seminary
Kansas City, Missouri

Snehlata Patel
Retired Pastor
Brooklyn, New York

Emerson B. Powery
Professor of New Testament
Messiah College
Grantham, Pennsylvania

Clayton Smith
Pastoral Staff
Church of the Resurrection
Leawood, Kansas

Harold Washington
Professor of Hebrew Bible
Saint Paul School of Theology
Kansas City, Missouri

Carol Wehrheim
Curriculum Writer and Editor
Princeton, New Jersey

IMMERSION BIBLE STUDIES

A fresh new look at the Bible, from beginning to end,
and what it means in your life.

Welcome to IMMERSION!

We've asked some of the leading Bible scholars, teachers, and pastors to help us with a new kind of Bible study. IMMERSION remains true to Scripture but always asks, "Where are you in your life? What do you struggle with? What makes you rejoice?" Then it helps you read the Scriptures to discover their deep, abiding truths. IMMERSION is about God and God's Word, and it is also about you—not just your thoughts, but your feelings and your faith.

In each study you will prayerfully read the Scripture and reflect on it. Then you will engage it in three ways:

Claim Your Story
> Through stories and questions, think about your life, with its struggles and joys.

Enter the Bible Story
> Explore Scripture and consider what God is saying to you.

Live the Story
> Reflect on what you have discovered, and put it into practice in your life.

IMMERSION makes use of an exciting new translation of Scripture, the Common English Bible (CEB). The CEB and IMMERSION BIBLE STUDIES will offer adults:

- the emotional expectation to find the love of God
- the rational expectation to find the knowledge of God
- reliable, genuine, and credible power to transform lives
- clarity of language

Whether you are using the Common English Bible or another translation, IMMERSION BIBLE STUDIES will offer a refreshing plunge into God's Word, your life, and your life with God.

1.

Prophecies of Judgment Against the Nations

Isaiah 1–10; 13–23; 28–31; 36–39

Claim Your Story

Have you ever known a saint? If the immediate image that comes to mind is an extraordinarily selfless or dedicated person—for example, Bishop Desmond Tutu or Mother Teresa—your answer might be no. If you think of the way Scripture describes a saint, however, then the answer is a definite yes!

The apostle Paul describes saints, in essence, as all who feel called into relationship with God and who seek to live out that relationship with integrity. While the Old Testament writers use a somewhat different vocabulary, they too speak of this basic concept, usually in terms of God's covenant with us.

For Isaiah, being right with God involved living according to God's desires, in other words, living a holy (or saintly) life. Looking around your own congregation, you will see a number of ways that people express their commitment to God. Many volunteer their time to help others either around the church or in the world at large. Within this, some commit themselves to work for justice just as Isaiah called on the Judeans to do. Some work to build a meaningful worship experience through supplying music, dance, liturgical leadership, or even such basic items as flowers or a weekly bulletin. Some offer their presence to comfort or to teach others. There are countless other acts of service as well. A vital church produces those who venture outside the sanctuary walls to carry God's message of love and justice to others rather than being content to let the weekly sermon suffice as social action and spiritual nourishment.

Isaiah invites all of us to consider the gifts and talents that God has given to us and to use them for the communal good. He calls us to care about our neighbors, both close to home and around the globe. We have an opportunity, as Isaiah did, to commit ourselves humbly and in trust to do God's will in whatever way God chooses to use us. If we take that step, Isaiah promises, we will not only experience the fullness of God's grace for ourselves; but we will also be part of bringing it to the world.

Enter the Bible Study

This study on Isaiah, Jeremiah, and Lamentations covers significant events in Judah's history including the Syro-Ephraimitic war (735–732 B.C.), the Assyrian siege of Jerusalem (701 B.C.), and the fall to Babylonia in 587/586 B.C. These years were marked by struggles for political power and national security, as well as by injustice and oppression. The study of this history is important, in part, because it shows us how God is at work even in the worst times that human beings can devise.

The relevance for our own lives is striking when we consider some of the topics addressed by Scriptures from Judah's day: the misuse of power, the corruption of justice, and the danger of false religion and of greed, to name a few. Other topics, such as demonstrating undeserved love and establishing peace, are not as dominant but are just as important.

Behind all the historical events, however, hovers God who is the leading actor, primary audience, and ultimate judge of the drama. God's role in human life is the key reason Isaiah was so concerned about social justice and acts of trust as we see in the chapters highlighted for this session, Isaiah 1–10; 13–23; 28–31; and 36–39.

A Prophetic "Sampler"

The first chapter of Isaiah provides a sampler of the prophet's message to the Jewish people. The themes we find run throughout the rest of the book.

First, speaking bluntly, the prophet said that God was a faithful parent and the nation was a rebellious child. Even the barnyard animals had sense enough to know who provided for them, but God's people did not know where to turn for nurture and protection. Israel and Judah had forsaken and despised the Holy One. As a result, these nations were like a body that is wounded and bruised from head to toe (1:2-3, 6).

Comparing Jerusalem to Sodom and Gomorrah, the Lord then condemned the sacrificial system that was the backbone of their worship, lifting up instead repentance from evil, the pursuit of justice, and the defense of the helpless. Isaiah singled out orphans and widows for special concern. In the days before social service networks and programs, the widows and the orphans were among the poorest and most helpless of people. They were not, however, outside of God's concern.

Despite these problems, however, there was hope. For Isaiah, it mattered immensely that history is in God's hands. God's plan was unfolding, and one day all nations would stream to the mountain of the Lord (2:2). This would prove to be even better news for Judah.

Isaiah of Jerusalem

The Book of Isaiah as we have it comes from at least three different time periods. Chapters 1–39 are generally recognized as being original to the man we know as Isaiah, the great prophet who lived in Jerusalem, began his prophecy in 742 B.C., and addressed several kings during his lifetime. Chapters 30–35 and 40–55 (Second Isaiah) date from about 540 B.C. after the destruction of Jerusalem and the exile to Babylon. Chapters 24–27 and 56–66 date from the time after 537 B.C. when the return to Jerusalem began.

From the written evidence, we can determine several things about Isaiah. He was the son of Amoz and was active during most of the latter half of the eighth century B.C. He enjoyed immediate access to several kings: Uzziah, Jotham, Ahaz, and Hezekiah (1:1). He was an insider and functioned within the institutions of Judah. He was married to a woman who was a *nebi'ah*, a prophetess (8:3), and had children (7:3; 8:1-4). Isaiah 8:16 suggests that he had a group of followers.

Speaking for God

Isaiah's call is narrated in Isaiah 6. Dating this to the year that King Uzziah died (742 B.C.), the prophet described a vision of God that appeared to him in the Temple. Faced with the unspeakable holiness of God, Isaiah immediately recognized his own sinful inadequacy. "Mourn for me; I'm ruined! I'm a man with unclean lips, and I live among a people with unclean lips" (verse 5). The grace of God prevailed, however. A seraph touched Isaiah's lips with a coal and pronounced him cleansed from sin. For the first time, God spoke: "Whom should I send, and who will go for us?" (verse 8, NRSV). The plural refers to the entire divine assembly. God had taken the initiative to appear to Isaiah, to cleanse him, and to call him. Now, Isaiah responded to God's gracious invitation: "I'm here; send me" (verse 8).

The task that God assigned to Isaiah seemed futile and fatalistic at first glance (verses 9-13). He was to preach so that the people would become deaf and blind. As a result of his ministry, the Judeans would refuse to repent and be healed. We must interpret these words with care. God was not really calling Isaiah to drive the people farther away; rather, God recognized from the beginning the hard-heartedness of the people. God knew that, confronted by the prophet's message, they would choose not to change.

Problems of the Times

Part of the difficulty was that the land had experienced peace and prosperity for a while, which was relatively rare. Ironically, this led to some problems. As ready money became available, those who were more fortunate used their resources to increase their holdings. The elite were particularly greedy; and as the land fell into the hands of the few, the peasants lost both their holdings and their freedom. They were forced to become tenants, sharecroppers, or slaves (5:8-10).

The change in regard to land ownership referenced in Isaiah 5:8 was not only a major social change, but also a violation of a very important part of the law. Land was not supposed to be bought at all because it all belonged to Yahweh (Leviticus 25:23). Allotments of land were made to every family and were thought of as gifts of God. The right of each family to its own allotment was sacred, understood to be guaranteed by God. Land is as essential to life, they thought, as air to breathing. Thus, if the head of a family died or the family sank into poverty, the law provided that the nearest male kinsman must marry the widow and see that the land was redeemed from the person to whom a debt on it was owed. This system of land distribution was obviously eroding fast, with disastrous consequences. The nation would be punished for this and for all of its other failures, Isaiah said.

A National Crisis

Of course, there were political complications in Isaiah's time as well. The first account we read after the prophet's call describes an encounter with King Ahaz of Judah (7:1). At the time, Assyria, under the rule of Tiglath-pileser, was an international power of frightening proportions. In an attempt to resist the might of Assyria, a coalition of smaller nations was formed. When King Ahaz of Judah refused to join the united front, King Rezin of Aram (Syria) and King Pekah of Israel attacked Judah. Rezin and Pekah hoped to remove Ahaz from the throne of Judah and replace him with a more cooperative ruler (7:1-9).

In this time of crisis, God commanded Isaiah and his son Shear-jashub ("the remaining few will return") to visit the terrified Ahaz. The prophet found Ahaz at one of the water conduits of Jerusalem, presumably examining the water supplies of the city in preparation for a long siege.

Isaiah's message was one of encouragement. The enemy nations were led by mere mortals who were no match for the power of God. All that was required of Ahaz was to have faith in God rather than turning to Assyria for a military alliance. Isaiah even offered to produce a miraculous sign as confirmation of God's trustworthiness: "The Lord will give you a sign. The young woman is pregnant and is about to give birth to a son, and she will name him Immanuel" (7:14). The baby's name, Immanuel ("God is with us"), would be a sign of God's coming deliverance.

Nevertheless, Isaiah's message was hard for Ahaz (and others) to accept. Withdraw from any alliance with Assyria and trust God to

Across the Testaments

Isaiah 7:14 and Matthew 1:23

Christians have long read Isaiah 7:14 as a prophecy of the birth of Jesus. When Matthew (1:23) quotes these words, he uses the Greek word for "virgin;" although the Hebrew word here simply means "young woman." The prophet does not seem to be thinking of the Messiah, though. In context, he was probably referring to some name-less mother-to-be (perhaps his own pregnant wife or the wife of the king—compare 7:3 and 8:1-4). Of course, in a broader sense, Isaiah is predicting a sign of God's saving power; and Christ is that sign par excellence.

eliminate the invaders from the countryside? Many must have wondered, Would God protect the trade routes in the process? Would God rebuild the economy, putting commodities back into the bazaars and coins in the buyers' pockets? The question may not have been so much, Are we able to trust in God to protect us? but, Can we afford to?

Thinking of it this way, we see that Ahaz needed to hear Isaiah's message, not because he was king, but because he was human. For that reason, if no other, Isaiah's message still speaks to us as well.

God's Broken Heart

Running throughout Isaiah's messages to Ahaz, other leaders, and the people themselves is an urgent plea to stay in right relationship with God. The prophet has clear ideas about what a good relationship with the Creator entails, and these are repeated throughout Isaiah 1–39. Time and again, we encounter calls to justice, humility, trust, and sincere worship. Problems with God are marked by the *opposite* behavior in Judah and in other nations.

By harboring idol worship, arrogance, injustice, and insecurity, Judah has broken its covenant relationship with God (2:5-17; 5:8-10, 23; 22:18-20) and broken God's heart as well. Other nations are also guilty (9:8-9; 10:12; 13; 15; 23), but none hurt God as Judah did.

This shattered bond is poignantly described in Isaiah 5. The poem is written as a love song; but it quickly takes on double meaning, turning into something much more serious and disturbing. The farmer lovingly cares for his vineyard as the bridegroom cares for the bride, but the bride turns out to be faithless. Surprise, the vineyard turns out to be Israel and Judah (5:7), and the farmer turns out to be God! The startled hearers find themselves being asked to confirm the judgment that God has determined against them.

A Word of Hope

Why should this terrible judgment be pronounced against God's own people? Because they have failed to be true to the covenant obligation. God had expected something from them and had been disappointed. The disappointment is expressed in the wordplay (which is hard to recapture in translation) at the end of the poem (5:7). God looked for a community built on the foundation of justice (*mishpat*) but found instead a community based on violence or bloodshed (*mishpakh*). God looked for righteousness (*tsedaqah*) and instead heard a cry for help (*tse'aqah*).

Isaiah then pronounced judgment on the people and groups who had been responsible for the conditions that would inevitably lead to catastrophe for both Israel and Judah (5:9-15). The picture we get in his seven "woes" is of a society that had lost its way. A great gulf had opened up between rich and poor, while comfort and prosperity had led at last to an arrogance that casually disregarded the concepts and principles of faith (see 2:9-17). People continued to believe in God, but not a God who made any difference in daily life.

They would soon discover differently, though. Those who had been so greedy for land would experience the landlessness of exile. There would be no escape from God's judgment.

All that Judah stood to lose is vividly represented in an oracle addressed to the wealthy women of Jerusalem (3:16-24). In place of their finery and extravagance, there would be only the marks of slavery. Instead of perfume, there will be a disgusting odor. Instead of a sash, a rope. Instead of styled hair, shaved heads. Instead of expensive clothes, rags as mourning clothes. Instead of beauty, shame. In ancient manuscripts, the word *shame* is not in the text, which gives a striking result. In place of beauty, there would be absolutely nothing.

Yet, intermingled with these woes is a powerful message of hope. Throughout the book that bears his name, Isaiah brings God's promise of a new day, a time when all peoples will stream to God's holy mountain to live in justice and peace (2:1-4). Punishment will come for the foreign nations but so will grace. The land will become God's "pride and splendor," and all who live in it will be holy and cleansed (4:2-6). To the people, it will be as if a great light has shone in the darkness (9:2). Even Egypt and Assyria will worship God and join those who walk in God's way (19:19-24). As for the remnant of Judah, they will not only be brought home (10:20-23), God will grace them with glory, beauty, justice, and strength (28:5-6). Mourning and sadness will be replaced by singing and a joyful heart (30:29).

The Hebrew people expressed their confidence in God's ultimate goal whenever they sang Psalm 46 in the Temple. Tradition still links this psalm—which also shaped Luther's great hymn, *A Mighty Fortress*—to Isaiah's age:

> God is our refuge and strength,
>> a help always near
>>> in times of great trouble.
> That's why we won't be afraid
>> when the world falls apart,
>> when the mountains crumble into the
>>> center of the sea. . . .
> God is in that city. It will never crumble.
>> God will help it when morning dawns. . . .
> The LORD of heavenly forces is with us!
>> The God of Jacob is our place of safety.
>>>>> (Psalm 46:1-2, 5, 7)

May this be our confidence as well!

Live the Story

As we read about the problems in Isaiah's time, it may be a surprise to see so many similarities with today. We also wrestle with social justice and wonder what is right. The issues of health care, tax reform, and other political concerns are a reflection for Christians of what we personally believe is right according to God's covenant call. We struggle with issues of humility and trust as well, both individually and as a nation. At some level we do believe that we are better than certain other people or countries, and we also feel more comfortable at times putting our trust in our own plans rather than God's. In that regard, we can see how the issue of idolatry, what we trust or value more than God, is still with us today. Even worship has become a source of contention: Should it be traditional or modern? Must it be on Sunday, or are other days okay? What about worship in homes or other locations on a regular basis? Is a church building necessary? These are some of the questions we face, and at their heart lie the questions Isaiah raised: What really pleases God, and how willing are we to let God's desire shape our choices?

Isaiah reminds us that God is still calling the church to make disciples, and God still instructs those disciples to live out their Christian commitment in the world. We are to live out our faith wherever we go, be it at home or in the workplace, school, the voting booth, or even the grocery store. Beyond that, we are to extend our love into the whole world, caring for the quality of life of all others, just as God does.

As we consider the church as a modern vineyard, we might ask, What response have we made to the loving care and concern of the Divine Gardener? What have we done to help nurture the young, tender vines? What fruits are we bearing to the world?

2.

Prophecies in Favor of Israel

Isaiah 11–12; 24–27; 32–35

Claim Your Story

Isaiah would certainly be perplexed by our modern proverb, "Politics and religion don't mix." From his viewpoint, politics and religion not only mixed, they were identical. One's true religious faith was reflected in one's political policy, and political actions were ultimately the result of one's religious convictions.

When we shift from consideration of Isaiah's conditions to our own present situation, the significance of corporate responsibility is even more intense. Unlike Isaiah's contemporaries, we have a voice in our national government. We elect our own presidents, prime ministers, and legislators. We can write to our political representatives and support lobbying organizations. We can give or withhold campaign funds. Both as individuals and as members of the church, we have a voice in our own government. How much more, then, will we be held responsible for our nation's actions? How much more should we take Isaiah's message to heart?

Of course, there are other forces besides government and political powers whose actions have deep and lasting effects on entire communities. Large factories, national and multinational corporations, labor unions, fraternal societies, and consumer groups all wield influence for good or evil. In each area, one needs to consider where responsibility lies for the actions of the organization. Who ultimately makes decisions and who is ultimately responsible?

For example, how much control rests in the hand of the individual who owns stock in a corporation that pollutes the environment? Or, in another example, how much influence does one member of a labor union have in securing justice for union and nonunion workers? If a consumer supports a company by purchasing its product, is the consumer responsible when that company moves its factory to a third-world country where it can hire labor at starvation wages and avoid health and safety restrictions?

The texts for this session offer beautiful words of hope and promise, but they also challenge us to consider what it means to live faithfully as we wait for God's plan to come to fruition. In our complex society, it is virtually impossible to live without entanglement in injustice in some area. What might God have us do differently right now?

Enter the Bible Study

The chapters covered in session one contain quite a few negative oracles against Judah and other nations. Here in session two, we will consider Isaiah's prophecies in favor of God's people as found in Chapters 11–12; 24–27; and 32–35. These chapters affirm that, while it is important to recognize the serious consequences of our individual and corporate sin, the biblical message contains more. The full story includes hope, promise, and a wonderful reason to repent: the unfailing grace and steadfast love of God. At the heart of the passages considered in this session is the promise that God is doing a new thing. God is preparing the world for a new place, a new Jerusalem that will provide a safe and abundant home for Judah in the future. For now, while they wait the people will have to suffer, but it will be worth it.

The harsh part of these visions for many of us lies in the brush clearing that God will do to make way for the new city. Nations will be destroyed; human beings will be wiped away. As Isaiah saw it, though, this was necessary. God's people could not truly be safe as long as their enemies existed. Thus these chapters intertwine beautiful visions of the age to come with horrible prophecies of devastation.

On a happier note, we see that the new home for God's people will be filled with all the aspects of covenant living lifted up in session one. There will be justice and righteousness (32:1-8), true worship in which all join (12:1-3; 27:7-13), and peace and security (11:10-16; 25:6-10a; 35:5-10). As two passages describe it:

> On this mountain,
>   the LORD of heavenly forces
>   will prepare for all peoples
>   a rich feast, a feast of choice wines,
>   of select foods rich in flavor,
>   of choice wines well refined.
> He will swallow up on this mountain
>   the veil that is veiling all peoples,
>   the shroud enshrouding all nations.
> He will swallow up death forever.
> The LORD God will wipe tears
>   from every face;
>   he will remove his people's disgrace
>   from off the whole earth,
>   for the LORD has spoken.
>
> (25:6-8)

> Then justice will reside in wild lands,
>   and righteousness
>   will abide in farmlands.
> The fruit of righteousness
>   will be peace,
>   and the outcome of righteousness,
>   calm and security forever.
> Then my people will live
>   in a peaceful dwelling,
>   in secure homes,
>   in carefree resting places.
>
> (32:16-18)

No wonder the people will sing out in thanksgiving (12:4-6; 24:14-16a; and so on)! Moreover, Judah will be restored for a purpose. A truly beautiful vineyard now, its fruit will fill the whole world (27:2-6). There is even a sense that creation itself will be restored through the new Zion in that all creation will see God's glory and experience God's healing (35:1-6a).

Starting Over

Isaiah 10 ends with the drastic image of Jerusalem chopped down and laid low (verses 33-34). Out of this felled people, however, shall grow something new, wonderful, and unexpected. "A shoot will grow up from the stump of Jesse," proclaims Isaiah 11:1. The reference is to a new king, a descendant of David, who will be a king as God intends, not someone like the past few generations of royalty in Israel and Judah. "The LORD's spirit will rest upon" the new king (11:2), which here refers to the "wind" or "breath" of God that brings strength, power, and courage to kings (see, for example, 1 Samuel 11:6 and 16:13-16). Filled with divine wisdom, this king will be a "Wonderful Counselor" and a "Prince of Peace" (Isaiah 9:6), under whom justice and righteousness will be restored to the kingdom (11:3-5).

The messianic implications of this true shepherd-king are expanded in Isaiah 11:6-9. There we see that all creation will be transformed during this king's rule to a place of peace and harmony, "The earth will surely be filled with the knowledge of the LORD" (11:9). Both human society and the natural world will be marked by an absence of violence and domination. What's more, the gift of this newness will extend to the nations and to the Hebrew people scattered across the known world (verses 10-11). This king from the line of David will bring home remnants of both Israel and Judah, forging them into one people once again. All will be brought back to the land, as once God brought them from Egypt (verses 12-16).

Isaiah believed that God's covenant with David (2 Samuel 7), that a king from his line would always be on the throne, would hold true. Isaiah had in mind an earthly king who either lived or was to come in his own time period. Isaiah understood him to be a human being through whom God would work. Looking back on these texts, the Christian church has seen connections to Jesus as the one who embodies these promises. The emphasis on peace, the restoration of creation, the cosmic implications, and the promise of homecoming all fit with Jesus' life and ministry. Many churches lift up and celebrate these themes in the liturgy used during the Lord's Supper, especially in the reassurance that one day "People will come from east and west, north and south, and sit down to eat in God's kingdom" (Luke 13:29).

Notably, this section of Isaiah concludes with the words of a doxology that Judah will sing in the future (Isaiah 12:1-11). This song of thanksgiving vibrates with the gifts of God to come: forgiveness, comfort, salvation, and joy. The prophet sings of the future deliverance as if it is already done. God has promised it so it is a sure thing. Punishment will come but so will restoration to a life better than before. In the face of such good news, the prophet and the people cannot help but sing!

A Cosmic Event

Isaiah 24–27 contains a prophetic apocalypse that speaks of a coming day of the Lord when the old world will be destroyed and a newly created order will be established. Following the usual pattern of apocalyptic literature, the vision is cosmic; it foresees changes to both heaven and earth.

The section begins with the terrible devastation wrought by God, who now chooses to unmake creation rather than allow the people to continue in their sin and guilt. Only the last verse offers a bit of hope: "On that day" (24:21), God will dwell in Jerusalem (verse 23). Isaiah then sweeps us up in rousing praise and thanksgiving to God. Looking ahead to the day when God acts, the prophet celebrates the destruction of cities that represent selfish indifference and arrogant exploitation. In place of these unjust societies will come a God-based community offering refuge and shelter to the poor and needy (25:1-5). This community, gathered on and around the mountain of God, will be blessed with peace and abundance (25:6-10a). With language later echoed in Revelation, we read of a rich feast, the destruction of death, and an end to all tears. On that day the people will say at last, "This is the LORD, for whom we have waited; let's be glad and rejoice in his salvation" (25:9). Notice, however, that while

About the Scripture

A Word About Moab

Isaiah 25:10b slips in a negative word about Moab. In contrast to those who live and celebrate on God's holy mountain, the Moabites will be humiliated and laid low. It is unclear why this oracle is included here and not among the other judgments against the nations in Chapters 13–23. It does, however, demonstrate that the unrighteous nations are doomed to destruction and stands in contrast to the promises for Judah in the preceding verses.

continuing the good news for Judah, the prophet manages to acknowledge current reality. The people are called to maintain their trust and hope in God's saving activity while in the midst of hard times.

The tension between future-oriented hope and present-lived experience is mirrored in the first two sections of Isaiah 26. Verses 1-6 are a hymn of praise to God, while verses 7-10 are a song of yearning of "the righteous" in Judah at the time who long for God's presence. The themes of hope and lament then continue to intertwine throughout the rest of the chapter, bringing in images from the Exodus. Much as on the last night in Egypt, when the angel of death passed overhead, the people are told to stay inside their homes "for in a little while the fury will be over" (verse 20).

The apocalyptic vision ends with some interesting images. First we read of God's victory over Leviathan (27:1). This great sea monster represents all the watery chaos that God overcame at creation (Genesis 1:2) and that still threatens life. The promise is that everything threatening to life, wholeness, and well-being will be eradicated.

Next, Isaiah describes Judah's future life with God in poetic imagery deliberately opposite to that in Isaiah 5:1-7. Where the earlier passage described Judah as a vineyard gone wild, here the vineyard is beautiful and blossoming. Guarded and tended by God, it produces fruit for the whole world (27:2-6).

In contrast to the vineyard, God will destroy an evil city (27:7-11). While the city is not named, it could refer to Samaria (the destroyed capital of Israel) or to a generic city representing all places of idolatry and corruption. The prophetic message closes with a promise of homecoming in Isaiah 27:12. In language reminiscent of Matthew 3:12, God will "beat grain from the channel of the Euphrates up to the Valley of Egypt." In this case, it is not to punish some and reward others. Isaiah says, "You will be collected, Israelites, one by one. . . . A great trumpet will be played. Those who were lost in the land of Assyria and those who were scattered in the land of Egypt will come. They will bow to the LORD at his holy mountain in Jerusalem" (verses 12-13). As Old Testament scholar Walter Brueggemann puts it, "The culmination of this visionary material is the proper worship of Yahweh in Yahweh's proper place of worship by Yahweh's most serious loyalists."[1]

Threats and Promises

Isaiah affirms that justice and righteousness will mark this new community inspired by "a spirit from on high" (32:15). Characterized by wisdom and kindness, God's people will now find peace, security, and rest within their society and with the surrounding world (verses 1-8, 15-20).

Yet, between these exciting visions of future blessings is a warning against complacency and indulgence (verses 9-14). As in Isaiah 3:16-26, the prophet addresses women. Here, however, they are not threatened with violent punishment; rather, they are called to leave their comfortable couches and actively lament for their country. "Strip yourselves, bare your skin, and tie mourning clothes around your waist, beating your breasts for the pleasant fields" (verses 11-12). Loss will proceed blessing, so mourning is appropriate.

The theme of blessing in the coming city of God then continues. God will bring security, salvation, wisdom, and knowledge (33:6). All the elements of a broken society from deserted, unsafe roads to blatant sins will be overturned and security will be restored (verses 7-16). God will come as a glorious king; and Jerusalem will become a holy place of unending health, worship, and joy (verses 17-24).

Following this, Isaiah returns to the harsh reality of the present world, which must be cleared away to make room for God's new realm. Chapter 34 wrenches us back to God's "day of vengeance" (verse 8) and the doom

About the Scripture

Lilith

Isaiah 34:14 contains the only biblical reference to *lilith*. It is unclear whether the text is using an obscure word for an unclean animal, or whether it indicates a female demon of a closely related name. Later Jewish folklore said Lilith was Adam's first wife.

that is to come. Edom is particularly singled out for vengeance. As in earlier oracles, the promised end is total devastation at the hands of the completely sovereign God.

Once all threats to God's people are removed, we see a joyous homecoming. We start with the transformation of nature itself. God is preparing a place for the returnees, and it is wonderful. Desert and wilderness now teem with plants (35:1-2), and Jerusalem itself is a place of healing. The weak and feeble find strength there, the fearful find courage, and those with disabilities find a cure (verses 3-6).

As for those who must make the journey home, God has provided for them as well. Unlike the Exodus from Egypt, there will be no wandering for forty years, no worry about survival. The returning exiles from Babylon will find a smooth road through a wilderness now filled with water and absent of dangerous beasts (verses 6b-9). Thus:

> The LORD's ransomed ones
>   will return and enter Zion
>   with singing,
>   with everlasting joy upon their heads.
> Happiness and joy
>   will overwhelm them;
>   grief and groaning will flee away.
>
> (verse 10)

What a glorious vision! The restoration of God's people is coming! Isaiah proclaims God's intention to create new heavens and a new earth where there will be gladness and rejoicing. In this new world, pain and suffering will be no more, and life will be long and fulfilling for the righteous.

We know, of course, that God's new order has not yet come into being. In the meantime, God's people are called to work for a better world. As we wait for this day to come, we can begin to participate in its blessings by striving for peace now. In this context, the time-honored words of St. Francis of Assisi seem as appropriate now as when they were written in the thirteenth century:

> Lord, make me an instrument of thy peace;
> where there is hatred, let me sow love;
> where there is injury, pardon;
> where there is doubt, faith;
> where there is despair, hope;
> where there is darkness, light;
> and where there is sadness, joy.[2]

God, grant that it be so!

Live the Story

Overall, peace was in short supply in Isaiah's time. The prophet presents a terrible portrait of Judah at the end of the eighth century B.C. We see a wide gap between "haves" and "have-nots," between an elite minority that held the reins of power and the disenfranchised majority that had no recourse to justice. We see one class of people luxuriating in wealth and overabundance while their neighbors struggled to scrape together the necessities of life. The prophet looks forward to a day when the poor will be judged with righteousness and the meek with equity (11:4), a day when all who take advantage of the status and helplessness of others will be treated in kind (24:2). That day had not come yet; however, and so he pleaded with the people of Judah to live faithfully in the meantime.

How should the church today respond to Isaiah's message? One approach would be to regard these passages as historic documents, chronicles of an unfortunate period somewhere in the distant past. From this point of view, these writings are valuable for their rhetorical power, their literary scope, and their influence on later writers of Scripture.

We might take another point of view, however. We might approach Isaiah's oracles as one might approach a mirror looking for reflections of our own society, our own errors, and our own predicament. In order to benefit from this perspective, we would need to ask searching questions such as: In what way is our society similar to the Judah of Isaiah's day? Does a small minority of people enjoy an abundant lifestyle while the majority lacks the basic necessities of life? How adept are we, as individuals and as a nation, at ignoring reality and deceiving ourselves? How skilled are we at disguising our idols, at dressing them up in respectable institutions and established traditions? How are we called to move forward in our relationships with God and with others? These are difficult questions that reach beyond the scope of this study. Nonetheless, it is questions such as these that move the study of Scripture from an academic exercise into a life-changing experience.

1. From *Isaiah 1–39*, by Walter Brueggemann, Westminster Bible Companion (Westminster John Knox, 1998); page 216.
2. From *The United Methodist Hymnal* (Copyright © 1989 The United Methodist Publishing House); 481.

3.

Prophecies of Israel's Deliverance

Isaiah 40–48; 58–66

Claim Your Story

"Tomorrow is another day."

"Things always get better if you just have faith."

"Time heals all wounds."

"When one door closes, God opens another."

What do you tell yourself when times are hard? What do you turn to for comfort? a pint of ice cream? a box of chocolates? your mother's chicken soup? We all have something that we hope will help us through dark nights and troubled times.

Even as a society, we know what it means to hope for a better day. We cling to promises that "prosperity is just around the corner." Across the political divide, we all anticipate a reduction in deficit spending and a rise in the employment rate. "Your vote matters," we say to one another, voicing our belief that a better day can come in the government through our collective efforts. At some level, we recognize there is a limit as to how much we should trust folk wisdom and political campaign slogans. But how much should we trust the promises of God?

Isaiah's answer is simple: We can trust God completely. Just as the Israelites could turn to God for comfort in their time of Babylonian bondage, so we can turn to God in times of distress. Knowing that God cares enough to be with us and to work for change on our behalf can help stabilize us mentally, emotionally, and spiritually. It helps us feel that we have a more solid footing on which to stand. In rough times, we hear again the good news that there is no need to be afraid (Isaiah 41:10, 13; 43:1-7; 44:8). God is with us, lifting us up and giving us strength until that better day arrives. The God who has carried us from infancy will continue to do so all the days of our lives (46:3-4). This is comfort, indeed!

Enter the Bible Study

In Isaiah 40–48 and 58–66, affirmations of joy and peace, renewal and redemption surge through times of suffering with a powerful note of hope. A better day is coming! God's people will be restored and, through them, all will be made right with the world. As mentioned in session one, Chapters 40–66 were not written by Isaiah of Jerusalem. Chapters 1–39 speak of conditions in the eighth century B.C. when the Assyrian Empire, ruthless and bent on expansion, had cast its shadow over everything. The tiny kingdom of Israel was crushed by this juggernaut in 721 B.C. while Judah survived as a little island surrounded by a hostile empire.

Chapters 40–55 reflect different conditions and are written in a different style. By the time this part of the book had been written, Assyria had been succeeded by Babylon, and Judah as a nation had been swallowed up by this new menace in 587 B.C. Jerusalem and the Temple had been destroyed and the better part of the population carried off into exile. These chapters were probably written toward the end of that period of exile (around 550–540 B.C.). The writer, known as Second Isaiah, saw that Cyrus of Persia was emerging as a new leader who would conquer Babylon, expand the empire, and then allow the exiles to go home.

Chapters 56–66 seem to come from a later time, so this section is commonly called Third Isaiah. The content fits into the difficult time of rebuilding after the exiles had returned to Jerusalem (approximately 450 B.C.).

As a means of accessing the message to two potentially different situations in Judah's life, we will focus on one chapter from each section that represents the whole. First we'll look at Isaiah 40 and its wonderful promise of comfort, followed by Isaiah 65 and its vision of the age to come.

A Timely Message

When Second Isaiah wrote to the people in exile, he sought to rouse them to new hope at the lowest period of their history. Many people by this time had ceased believing in God or doubted that God could make any difference in the world. They wondered if their defeat at the hand of Babylon proved that the foreign gods were, in fact, more powerful than God. Along with the grief of being forcibly expelled from their homeland and mourning over its destruction, they lamented the apparent loss of God in their lives. Now, however, there was danger that the people might go so far into despair that even God would be unable to bring them back again. In this situation, the wonderful words of God came to the unknown prophet: "Comfort, comfort my people" (40:1).

Comfort. What a soothing word! Down through the ages, musicians have written the concept into great works. Theologians have embraced the ideas as applying to God and God's Spirit. Advertisers have used the word to lure people into buying everything from shoes to mattresses. It is a word that elicits the thought of something good, and the "something good" for the Hebrew people was that God was about to provide a new way of life for them.

To underscore the care that the people will receive, the writer uses a favorite biblical image of God here: a shepherd. What a wonderful picture of encouragement for us as well! Notice the verbs: *feed, gather, carry,* and *lead* (verse 11, NRSV). The shepherd is the one who provides for the needs of the flock when they cannot provide for themselves. The shepherd is the one who cares for the weak, defenseless sheep when trouble of any kind approaches. The shepherd is the one who maintains order against divisive forces from within and against enemy forces from without. Strong, yet gentle—that is the image of God as Shepherd Comforter, an image that brought comfort to the people in Isaiah's day. It remains a beautiful picture of God for us.

Let the Journey Begin

At last came good news for the exiles: Jerusalem had "served her term, that her penalty is paid" (verse 2, NRSV). God was going to release the

About the Scripture

Reasons to Hope

This session specifically considers Isaiah 40–48 and 58–66. These chapters contain several ideas and images that offer hope and promise. For example:

- All that happens is at the hands of the Creator God, and this God is now doing a new thing (Isaiah 40:12-31; 42:5, 9-10; 43:15, 19; 44:24-28; 45:11-12, 18; 48:6-13; 65:17-25).
- There is no reason to fear (Isaiah 41:10, 13-14; 43:1-7; 44:8).
- Light will shine in the darkness (Isaiah 42:6-7; 58:8, 10; 60:1-3).
- God alone is God, and God alone can save (Isaiah 41:21-29; 43:11-13; 46:9-10; 48:12, 17).

Two of the most familiar images from these chapters are of a highway in the desert (40:3-5) and being able to fly on wings like eagles (40:31).

captives from bondage and provide a "new exodus" even grander than the first. Note that this long-awaited blessing would come *after* the free and gracious gift of God's forgiveness (verse 4), something God had been ready to offer from the beginning. Finally, however, the people were able to confess their wrongdoing and admit their need of forgiveness, so they could now receive it.

Thus the forgiving God came as the Deliverer, as the one who led the people along the highway back to their homeland. The two-pronged imagery of the former Exodus through the desert and the festival procession of the Babylonian gods along the great highway was not lost on the Judeans. Even so, we know many people balked at the idea of leaving the comfortable life they had. The road was long and the trip was difficult. Therefore, God provided Second Isaiah to give words of encouragement and strength to the faltering pilgrims. The way back would be made easier by a loving, caring God who would be seen in divine glory by the whole world!

The core of the prophet's affirmation is this: God is Lord of creation and Lord of history. God is above the world, firmly controlling all its powers (verses 21-41). God did not create and then let things go, leaving human beings at the mercy of unfolding events, subject to helplessness and futility.

God's purposes are being worked out. Thus the people can rejoice and look forward to a glorious renewal. As the text so eloquently puts it:

> those who hope in the LORD
> will renew their strength;
> they will fly up on wings like eagles;
> they will run and not be tired;
> they will walk and not be weary.
>
> (verse 31)

Moreover, God will do more than see the exiles safely home. God will be there to guard them against potential harm that might come from the journey or from future enemies. The promise given in Isaiah 43:1b-3a is one that we continue to lift up in services of comfort today:

> Don't fear, for I have redeemed you;
> I have called you by name;
>   you are mine.
> When you pass through the waters,
>   I will be with you;
>   when through the rivers,
>   they won't sweep over you.
> When you walk through the fire,
>   you won't be scorched
>   and flame won't burn you.
> I am the LORD your God,
>   the holy one of Israel, your savior.

As proof of the divine power to protect and redeem, God was preparing to lift up a human instrument who would be a most unexpected savior—Cyrus of Persia, one of the most enlightened rulers of the ancient world. The Jewish people were particularly glad to see Cyrus overcome Babylon because it was his policy to allow exiled people to return to their homelands. Indeed, the policy was implemented by edict that same year.

Other rulers of the time commonly uprooted the leading citizens of con-quered territory and carried them off, believing that by so doing there was little possibility of strong leaders emerging that might stir up trouble. Cyrus believed that a stronger nation, free to worship its own gods and justly governed, would be a more stable part of the empire over the long haul. Thus, he not only allowed the Jews to go home and rebuild, but he also restored all the precious equipment plundered from the Temple.

Disappointed Expectations

Cyrus was a source of hope to all, and he is the only pagan ruler des-ignated in the Old Testament as servant of God. In a speech that starts in Isaiah 44:24, God says:

> I am the LORD. . . .
> who says of Cyrus, 'He is my
>   shepherd,
>   and he shall carry out all my
>   purpose';
> and who says of Jerusalem, 'It
>   shall be rebuilt,'
>   and of the temple, 'Your
>   foundation shall be laid.'
>
> (verses 24, 28, NRSV)

Even with Cyrus's support, however, the return did not prove easy, as Isaiah 65 hints. Judah had been devastated by Babylon's attack, and no one left behind had seen a reason to rebuild the city. Second Kings 24:14 reports that those who remained were "the poorest of the land's people."

Not all the exiles, by any means, had chosen to return. Many had become part of the Babylonian culture, successful in business and ready to remain as a tolerated Jewish colony.[1] Probably only a minority, the rigidly loyal ones, had the courage or even the desire to return. Those who returned would have high hopes, so it would be a disappointment to encounter the reality back home. The land was in shambles, other people had moved onto the ancestral lands, and no one was particularly happy to see the exiles come back. In fact, Ezra and Nehemiah record that those who returned met a fair amount of opposition from local groups to their efforts to rebuild. (See Ezra 4.)

The physical rebuilding was therefore very slow and difficult. Even more difficult was the rebuilding of faith. Why had God allowed the chosen people to be virtually destroyed? Cyrus died, and other rulers succeeded who were not as enlightened and were less flexible. The returned exiles wondered, Would the monarchy of David ever be restored? This was the group for whom Third Isaiah wrote.

Worth Waiting For

While some of the images in Isaiah 65 show the problems faced by the people (verses 1-16), others lift up a glorious vision of the ultimate restoration of God's people to joy and peace (verses 17-25). Verses 17-25 assure that more is about to happen than the rebuilding of Jerusalem. The "old" heavens and the "old" earth of Genesis 1 will be transformed and renewed. The Hebrew verb used here, *bara'*, means more than "create"; it emphasizes the initiation of something new, something never before seen. The passage emphasizes that God will do the creating.

Of course, when God initiates a new venture of any kind, with that venture comes change. Not to worry, though: "past events won't be remembered; they won't come to mind" (verse 17). God, through the prophet, reminds the people to let go of what they are holding so tightly, such as traditions or rituals, and to get out of those ruts. As a result of this change, the people will "be glad and rejoice forever" (verse 18). The joy of the people and the joy of having God in Jerusalem will make the city the center of true worship, a place where God is honored and sorrow is no more. What comforting words to hear: "No one will ever hear the sound of weeping or crying" (verse 19).

Applying these thoughts to the idea of change, the picture emerges as one of reconciliation, of soothing the fears that are caused by change. Even the foreign nations will be part of this new community. The passage then moves to promises of God that center around the length of one's life.

Memories of God's Deliverance

Matthew 3:3, Mark 1:3, Luke 3:4, and John 1:23, which occur within the accounts of the ministry of John the Baptist in the wilderness, echo the words of the prophet in Isaiah 40:3: "A voice cries out, 'In the wilderness prepare the way of the LORD, make straight in the desert a highway for our God' " (NRSV). Isaiah's words promise God's deliverance from exile in Babylon in phrases that evoke memories of the Exodus. These memories of deliverance from Egypt and from Babylon added power and depth to the early church's understanding of God's work of deliverance through Jesus Christ.

Those in the better day will now live a long, full, and abundant life as a sign of divine favor (verse 20).

Home at Last

Long life was not the only thing God promised. Home ownership and productive vineyards were also part of the plan. Think about the people who heard these words. These were the descendants of people who escaped Pharaoh's torment by fleeing Egypt and dragging their tents and possessions all over the wilderness for forty years. No time to build a house when the movement of the cloud by day or the pillar of fire by night was so uncertain. There was only time to gather the children and livestock, fold up the tent, and follow God's leading. There was no time to plant vineyards, much less wait for the vines to produce fruit, only time for a quick meal of manna and quail.

The move into the Promised Land brought little or no security as the Hebrews adapted to the Canaanite culture. Some big power, Assyria or Egypt or another foreign country, was always invading and altering the status of God's people. Now God promised that life would be secure. There would be time to build houses and to "live in them" (verse 21). The vineyards would not only be planted, but also the wait for the production of the grapes implied longevity on the land. The people knew about lack of security; their joy now centered on the ability to "make full use of their handiwork" (verse 22).

The promise was one of "settling in," of attaining a home place and possessing land. No more exilic existence. No more foreign invaders. No more fruitless efforts. Things were looking up for God's people. The picture is one of an idyllic existence in a joyful, productive, stable environment— a life where work would no longer be destroyed by war and conquest, and where families would live as blessed by God. Yet there was more!

God's presence would be so near that before the people called, God would hear and answer (verse 24). While they were still thinking about asking God for something, God would perceive their needs and respond according to the divine purpose. Even if the request came in the middle of a spoken sentence, God would be readily accessible. God would no longer be silent, but God's blessing would extend to the very thoughts of their consciousness. It was a glorious vision, indeed!

Live the Story

As we consider Isaiah's words of comfort to the people in exile, we can see areas of life where we ourselves might bring comfort and peace to others. These Scripture passages encourage us to look for ways to bring "a better day" to those around us. In the workplace or at school, for example, we can opt to glorify God through seeking to build an atmosphere of peaceful harmony. Perhaps there is a coworker or fellow student under stress who could use a bit of help or just a listening ear. Comfort can come in many forms.

In community situations, a kind word, a bit of flexibility, a neighborly concern for those in the same building, on the same block, or around the same part of town can promote and encourage good will and peaceful coexistence. Opportunities abound for clothes closets, food pantries, and financial aid to help people pay rent and utility bills. For an individual or family in need, these charities represent more than "comfort"; they are a gift of life. Our homes present a chance to provide comfort to others as well. Even a household of one person can be a place where family members and friends find a restful haven.

"Do not be afraid," says God through the voice of the prophet, over and over again (41:10, 13-14; 43:1-7; 44:8). Do not be afraid to reach out to others. Do not be afraid to speak up for what is right. Do not be afraid to open your hearts in compassion, your hands in generosity, and your arms in loving embrace. Within the gift of comfort you have received from God, do not be afraid to extend comfort when the opportunity presents itself. A new day is coming, a better day, when God will create new heavens and a new earth where there will be gladness and rejoicing. In this new world, pain and suffering will be no more, and life will be long and fulfilling for the righteous. Until that day arrives, what will you do to bring comfort to those who need it?

1. From *Understanding the Old Testament*, by Bernhard W. Anderson (Prentice-Hall, 1986); page 516.

Prophecies of the Messiah

Isaiah 49–57

Claim Your Story

A child is born to us,
  a son is given to us,
  and authority will be on his shoulders.
He will be named
  Wonderful Counselor, Mighty God,
  Eternal Father, Prince of Peace.

(Isaiah 9:6)

He was pierced
  because of our rebellions
  and crushed because of our crimes.
He bore the punishment
    that made us whole;
by his wounds we are healed. . . .
He was oppressed and tormented,
  but didn't open his mouth.
Like a lamb being brought to slaughter,
  like a ewe silent before her shearers,
  he didn't open his mouth.

(Isaiah 53:5, 7)

These quotes from the Book of Isaiah have resonated within the faith community for centuries as meaningful texts within which we see

descriptions of our Lord Jesus Christ. As you think back over the generations, can you imagine how many Christians have been moved by these
passages? How many times have we heard these words read during Advent
or Lent? They are part of a worship experience that runs deep in our history and our identity as followers of the Messiah. When we look to the sections in Isaiah that, for Christians, shed light on the person and mission of
Jesus, we see how God has acted on our behalf in the past and continues
to do so now. We see how the presence of the living Lord, for us identified as the Risen Christ, provides both consolation and strength during
the painful experiences of life. Best of all, we find in the promise of the
world to come a reason to hold onto hope.

The quote from Isaiah 53 comes from Isaiah's fourth servant song. It
is especially meaningful for Christians. Perhaps part of why we gravitate
to this passage lies in the way it lifts up suffering as part of the Servant's
mission. We look for the reassurance that comes from knowing our own
punishment has been borne by another, but we also seek understanding in
relation to the suffering we find in life. Is there a way that our suffering can
be redeemed? Does it matter if we suffer for others? And where is God in
the midst of what we endure?

Enter the Bible Story

We now turn to images of the Messiah in Isaiah 49–57. These chapters contain three of the four Servant Songs written by Second Isaiah and
addressed to the community in exile (42:1-4; 49:1-6; 50:4-9; 52:13–53:12).
No one knows for sure whom the writer had in mind; and, as we will see,
the servant's identity seems to shift from chapter to chapter.

Before we begin, though, perhaps a word should be said about the setting of the songs. Isaiah 49–57 speak of God's great love for the people
and of the divine goal to restore them. Although there are oracles against
corrupt leaders (56:9-12) and idolatry (57:1-13), much of the text is good
news. God is ready to redeem the people and intends to restore them
(49:7-26; 50:1-3).

This salvation for God's children will be a new exodus and perhaps a
return to a new Eden (51:1-16; 55:12-13). Jerusalem has suffered enough;

even mountains and trees will celebrate God's victory (55:12). On that day, God will call the people to a great feast (55:1-2); and all will be welcome on God's holy mountain (56:3-7). There, people will experience God's healing, comfort, and peace (57:16-19). This is the promise that surrounds the Servant Songs of Isaiah.

A Light to the Nations

Isaiah 49:1-6 introduces a "servant" who may be either an individual or the people themselves. This passage lifts up God's sense of purpose in the world alongside God's power to create. The servant speaks of God's call in verse 1: "The LORD called me before my birth, called my name when I was in my mother's womb." In verse 6, the servant's understanding of God's power unfolds in rapid succession. God is the one who creates. God has a purpose for good for all nations. God calls people to become involved with God's purposes. The servant accepts God's role for the nation of Israel. The mission to be a "light to the nations" (verse 6) may seem futile, but it will be achieved. Through the servant, God's salvation will "reach to the end of the earth" (verse 6). The servant recognizes that God is his source of strength (verse 5).

A Teacher Who Trusts God

The servant reappears in Isaiah 50:4-11 as a teacher who sustains the people with his words and as a learner who listens in order to be taught (verse 4). God is the source of knowledge. We also read that the servant has been violently attacked (verse 6), yet the servant does not complain. He declares, "The Lord GOD helps me" (verse 7, NRSV). The passage communicates a tone of deep confidence and trust in God's vindication. His suffering was not in vain, and God's purposes are at work. In fact, the servant offers sharp challenges: "Who will contend with me? Let us stand up together. Who are my adversaries? Let them confront me. It is the Lord GOD who helps me" (verses 8-9, NRSV). Four repetitions of the divine name of God in verses 4-9 emphasize the servant's recognition of God's presence and power. This servant song sets the stage for the images of the servant in Isaiah 52:13–53:12.

The One Who Suffers

The final Servant Song (Isaiah 52:13–53:12) is the one best known to Christians. This passage flings us headlong into a consideration of what it means to suffer. We are not talking here about "suffering" inconvenience when the electricity goes off, the hot water runs out, the telephone lines are down, or any of the push-button appliances fail. We are talking about real suffering, the kind that changes people. Sometimes it makes them bitter and complaining. Sometimes the experience of realizing how frail and vulnerable they are makes people more humble or grateful just to be alive. Often it makes people more compassionate and more caring.

Certainly, in this song, the suffering of the Servant served a purpose; although it was hard to see at first. Unattractive and seemingly insignificant, he appeared to be just a standard, run-of-the-mill person whose entire lifespan was marked by suffering. Someone without beauty, this individual would have been overlooked by most in society. The "man who suffered, who knew sickness well" (53:3) was so physically unattractive that people turned their heads to avoid looking at this repulsive visage. Painful as this would have been, we read further: "He was despised and avoided by others" (verse 3). We may wonder why. What had he done to deserve such horrible treatment? Yet again, Isaiah states that the Servant was despised and people didn't think about him (verse 3). The eventual answer as to why this man suffered is not what we anticipate: "It was certainly our sickness that he carried, and our sufferings that he bore" (verse 4). The Servant suffered for the sins of others. Scripture says "*our* sickness . . . *our* sufferings . . . *our* rebellions . . . *our* crimes" (verses 4-5, italics added). Make no mistake about this Servant's suffering—the suffering resulted from what others had done. The sufferer was not the sinner, nor was the sinner the sufferer; and the first-person plural pronouns *we* and *our* make the involvement personal for the people addressed by these words.

Christians traditionally describe Jesus Christ and his ministry with these words from Isaiah. We think of Jesus as the one who was indeed "pierced because of our rebellions" (verse 5). Whether the prophet was actually looking that far ahead, we do not know. At times what seems to have been in his mind was a picture of an apocalyptic figure who would come soon and transform the meaning of suffering for everyone. At times the prophet seems to have been calling on the people of Israel themselves, challenging them to use the hard experience they had been through to bring a blessing to all peoples of the earth.

The servant suffered for others, and through this vicarious suffering came a restoration of health. The passage asserts that his punishment "made us whole" and that "by his wounds we are healed" (verse 5). As before, notice the *us* and *we* here. The voice has shifted again from that of Second Isaiah alone to that of the entire community of those who experienced the wholeness that resulted from the suffering: "Like sheep we had all wandered away, each going its own way, but the LORD let fall on him all our crimes" (verse 6). The unattractive, even repulsive-looking Servant, the insignificant one, suffered for others—for the *we*, *us*, and *our* of humankind.

The text continues by outlining in vivid detail exactly how the suffering servant was "oppressed and tormented" (verse 7). Treated harshly and unjustly, he never uttered a word in defense or retaliation. Instead, the servant remained silent, submissive, as quiet as the lamb led to slaughter or the sheep being shorn. We see here no fight, no agitation, no anxiety— just an eloquent condemnation represented by total silence.

As the text in Isaiah describes how the servant suffered, we begin to expect some signs of public sympathy. Surely now people would step forward in some sort of rescue effort for this poor, defenseless person. But no—the response was total lack of concern, abandonment to the fullest degree. No one even tried to turn aside the condemnation, execution, and dishonorable burial. We might almost expect at this point to hear the servant cry out, "Why me?" Abandoned in death as in life when he had done nothing wrong, how is the Servant to find peace? Certainly he had not received justice.

Isaiah 53:10-12 then reveals the purpose behind the pain; because the servant took on the punishment due to others, he will become the means through which "The LORD 's plans will come to fruition through him" (verse 10). God has caused this suffering, not as a penalty, but as the vicarious substitute for the actual guilty ones. The servant has become the means by which they will be made righteous (verse 11). He bore the iniquities as an agent of God's work of reconciliation, not because the suffering was deserved, but because God's purpose was somehow wrapped up in his tragic life, death, and burial. Vindication for the servant does come at last, along with restitution. The servant will see offspring, enjoy prolonged life and prosperity, and have a portion with the "great."

A Transformed Community

In the experience of exile, the people of Israel suffered as they had never suffered before, not just in loss of life and possessions, but in being uprooted and carried off to make a new beginning in a strange culture. For them, it was a terrible experience of landlessness, and landlessness meant that they had lost God's blessing. Even the name of the God they worshiped was not known in Babylon. The exile, therefore, was not only a physical catastrophe, but also a psychological and religious disaster of staggering significance. Everything they had counted on had failed them. How could their belief in God survive such a terrible blow?

Those who first read the Fourth Servant Song must have felt that the prophet's message put all their recent tragic experience into a new and positive perspective. "God is not dead," Second Isaiah seemed to be saying, "but is still the Lord of creation and of history. It is time now for a brave new affirmation of faith." Suffering, according to this startling new interpretation, could no longer be viewed as a simple matter of retribution. Suffering was also part of God's plan, a means by which God's blessing could become real to people who had never really known God.

For a Judean in exile, this perspective could potentially change everything. We can imagine some saying, "If this is so, we have to change our attitude completely toward people who suffer. Using the old theology, we have all been judgmental and harsh. We have missed what God is really doing in the world. We have despised the true servant of God and rejected him. We have believed that the servant was getting what he deserved, and we stood by self-righteously. What a terrible mistake we have made, for the servant was altogether innocent and his suffering was for us!"

The Gospels and the Birth of a Messiah

Three other passages in Isaiah are traditionally associated with the Messiah. Matthew 2:23 quotes the Immanuel promise in Isaiah 7:14. The "Wonderful Counselor" promise in Isaiah 9:6, while not quoted in the New Testament, offers deep meaning for Christians. However, Matthew 4:15-16 picks up the language in Isaiah 9:1-2. "The shoot of the stump of Jesse" promise in Isaiah 11 echoes in the New Testament accounts placing Jesus in the house of David. (See Matthew 1:1-17; 2:2; Luke 1:32-33; 3:23-28; Romans 15:13; Revelation 22:16.)

Scholars differ as to whether these prophecies in Isaiah originated during the reigns of Ahaz and Hezekiah or later when Judah had already become an Assyrian province. For our reflection, the date really doesn't make much difference; the important fact is that Isaiah anticipated the birth of a messianic child. His expectation appears to develop from the announcement of Immanuel's birth in Isaiah 7 to an enlarged understanding of a divine Son (9:6) who would carry in his hand the redemption of all Israel and, indeed, of the world (11:4, 9).

As the empire of David and Solomon crumbled and Assyria encroached on their borders, the people of Israel began to despair of receiving a human Messiah to deliver them from their political and military enemies. It was in this period that the Book of Isaiah was written including visions of a Messiah who is both "Mighty God" (9:6) and heir to the throne of David. After the fall of Jerusalem and the Babylonian exile, the possibility of restoration of the Davidic Empire seemed still more improbable. So the messianic hope became increasingly projected into the distant future and associated with the end of time.

What a discovery this was! The implications could have changed the whole course of Israel's religion. What would happen if the covenant community really lived up to its calling to be the servant of God in the world? What if, instead of complaining, they quietly accepted pain as a means of bringing the blessing of God to others, for example to pagan peoples who in the past they had seen only as enemies? What if, like the servant, those in exile were able to be faithful and to leave everything in God's hands? What if, to serve God, they were willing to undergo death. And what if, in faithfulness and love, they were willing to die in the place of those whose failures deserved the punishment never measured out to them? What witness and message might that bring to the world? In the realm of faith, such suffering is not the end of the road and the negation of hope; it is the beginning of something new.

With the benefit of hindsight, we know the people as a whole never really shared Second Isaiah's vision of what the acceptance of suffering could mean. Neither, perhaps, did they even understand it. Still, the word of God never returns to God empty-handed (55:11). It takes hold in the hearts of human beings and becomes real in their lives. Even this prophet, however, could not have realized how magnificently this idea would find its home in the life of a poor peasant from Galilee.

The Message for Today

God chose the Servant to suffer without retaliation or even without explanation in order to bring about the total restoration of health and well-being for others. The one who suffered alienation from family, rejection from the community, and separation from God also suffered hopelessness and utter dejection. Into the reality of this passage come many people today who accept undeserved suffering and sorrow without complaint. Perhaps the accepting ones are greatly outnumbered by those who lament their fate by lashing out at those around them, by proclaiming their innocence and disclaiming their need for punishment. Still, almost everyone's memory contains the image of at least one quietly accepting soul, whose faith in God's sovereignty transcends the pain and agony of the moment.

Pain and agony can also be reflected in those who take the consequences of their loved ones' mistakes upon themselves. What mother has not yearned to "take up for" her child whose poor study habits left insufficient time to complete the project only to stand aside while the child suffered the consequences? What father has not wanted to provide all the material possessions of comfort to the young adult fired for poor performance only to stand aside while the person struggled with the realities of the working world?

We know, of course, as did Second Isaiah, that the innocent do suffer. Many people experience unfair treatment by those in authority, those who make decisions about a promotion, positive change in location, or a raise.

Many are aware of oppression and injustices in today's society but feel helpless in combating or correcting these evils. Many who do speak out, especially in countries with limited freedom, suffer unspeakable atrocities over which they have no control. A minor offense can be multiplied into a life sentence. Dissidents are jailed and forgotten. Modern prophets are exiled into oblivion. Human rights can be subtly undermined and thus reduced to nothing.

For Christians, the Suffering Servant helps us understand the Suffering Savior, who suffered for *our* transgressions for what *we* deserved to reconcile *us* to the God whose purpose was demonstrated for the salvation of the world. Scripture states that "All have sinned and fall short of God's glory" (Romans 3:23), and that "The wages that sin pays are death, but God's gift is eternal life in Christ Jesus our Lord" (Romans 6:23). Today's believer, with grateful acknowledgment of the Suffering Savior, responds, "Amen, so be it."

Live the Story

As we ponder on Isaiah's descriptions of the role of the Servant and how Christians apply these descriptions to God's work through Jesus, we remember again all of the New Testament messages of what the Messiah has accomplished for the world. In Jesus we have new life, and we have it abundantly. Building upon God's promises to the Hebrew people, we have forgiveness of sins and the promise of a new age to come. In such contemplation, questions arise about suffering, the divine presence, and life after death. What difference, if any, does it make that we can read Isaiah in light of Christian hope?

About the Scripture

The First Servant Song

The first Servant Song, not covered in this session, is in Isaiah 42:1-4. The servant is described as God's delight. He is chosen by God, God's spirit dwells in him, and he will bring justice to the earth. While the servant is not identified, he may be a king of Judah who will reign as David did, restoring the nation to its former glory and goodness.

Surely our belief in resurrection must affect, to some degree, the way in which we read these texts and apply their meaning to our lives.

Most of us look forward to a future time, as Isaiah did, when all wrongs will be made right and all sorrow will end. The promise of an afterlife does not negate the pain from tragedies in this world, although it does offer some comfort and hope. The pain we experience in the here-and-now is genuine, and it can lead us to feel as helpless as did the Judeans in exile. There is no shame in this. Belief in an afterlife may be cause for hope; but it offers no shield from, nor explanation of, human suffering. We still struggle with anger, hurt, and confusion when calamity strikes; and we are forced to keep seeking the answers as to why such things happen. We take heart the words of Jesus in John 16:22: "You have sorrow now; but I will see you again, and you will be overjoyed. No one takes away your joy." In Jesus the Messiah we find that God is present with us in the midst of suffering, and that God grants us the strength to endure. We do not have to wait until a return from exile or the advent of an afterlife for God's healing and supportive presence. God is with us now, thanks be to God!

Christians live in this hope. No matter what happens, we find ways to practice this hope day by day in all that we do and experience; and we share this hope with others.

5.

Jeremiah's Call and His Warnings to Judah

Jeremiah 1–25

Claim Your Story

Think about the last time you were in a worship service. Did you come out feeling better? Hopefully the answer is yes. Most of us go to worship to strengthen our connection to God, deepen our faith, and renew our commitment to ministry. When this happens as it usually does, we do indeed feel better about ourselves and about life in general.

What happens, though, when feeling better becomes the only goal, with no thought to serving God or others once we leave the sanctuary? What happens when the worship experience becomes a means of justifying self-centered complacency or worse, non-loving treatment of others? These were some of the questions that Jeremiah raised to the people of Judah. Because they were acting as he described, they were not happy to have their conduct and hypocrisy to light.

Perhaps you know of a modern "Jeremiah" who tries to follow God's call but meets with opposition. I think of a young woman who met hostility at every turn because of her determination to achieve a theological education. Many family members and friends told her that she could not be called to the ministry because she was a woman. After much thought and prayer, however, she decided to persevere. She is now an effective and much beloved pastor of a congregation, but the old wounds still hurt.

Or, we might think of "Jeremiahs" outside of the church setting. Do you know of anyone who has hit a roadblock while fighting for fairness in the face of job discrimination either in entry-level hiring practices or in promotion and monetary practices? What about someone who speaks out against multinational corporations that exploit indigenous labor in under-developed countries in order to make a larger profit on the world market, or someone who takes a stand for environmental concerns? Those who follow their conscience are not always appreciated for their efforts, especially by those who feel justified in maintaining their current practice.

Enter the Bible Study

Perhaps the most important date in the Old Testament is 587 B.C. We could say that everything written before that time points ahead to the catastrophe of the exile in Babylonia, and everything written afterward seeks to explain and interpret it. The long ministry of Jeremiah falls on both sides of that date, making him a unique figure in Israel's history, the hinge joining *what was* with *what came to be*.

Jeremiah 1–25 contains the account of Jeremiah's call and many of the warnings he delivered to Judah. One of the first things we notice in skimming these chapters is Jeremiah's use of allegory and metaphor. He describes Judah as a bride (2:2, 32), a vine (2:21), an unfaithful wife (3:1-14), and a harlot (4:30). The nation's fate is symbolized through such mundane objects as an almond tree branch (1:11), a loincloth (13:1-11), a wine jar (13:12-13), and a basket of figs (24:1-10). Perhaps the best-known imagery of these chapters is that of the potter and clay found in Jeremiah 18:1-12, which the apostle Paul recalls in Romans 9:20-24.

The Call and the Promise

Like many prophets, Jeremiah was not called during a time of peace. Indeed, Jeremiah 1:1-3 tells us that the word of the Lord came to Jeremiah on several occasions: in the days of King Josiah; again in the days of Josiah's son Jehoiakim; and throughout the reign of King Zedekiah, "until the fifth month of the eleventh year of King Zedekiah, Josiah's son, when the people of Jerusalem were taken into exile" (verse 3). By naming each of these kings, the text sets the stage for our interpretation of Jeremiah's call. He would bring God's message to a people on a collision course with doom.

About the Scripture

Finding the Heart of Jeremiah

We have the feeling that we know a great deal more about what Jeremiah thought and felt than we do about other prophets, but we really have limited material out of which to create a biography. Furthermore, the person of Jeremiah, like Moses and the prophets, is always subordinate to the message he carried. The prose sections of Jeremiah have generated the view that the material was shaped by editors who preserved Jeremiah's thought and enhanced it with the theological views emerging from the settings at a later time. More revealing about Jeremiah are the poems, which record the anguish, loneliness, and discouragement Jeremiah felt about his ministry and his emotional struggle with God. We feel as we read these that we are looking into his very soul! Yet we also note that the words of Jeremiah are shaped by the Psalms, that he reached for phrases from the traditional laments of his people to express his deepest feelings. Thus, while the real Jeremiah is to a certain extent revealed in his poetic words, he is also elusive, hidden behind them.

Thus, reading Jeremiah 1:1-3 is a bit like reading the end of a book first. We see the outcome of Jeremiah's call before we see the call itself. Whoever put this section in its final form—whether it was Jeremiah, his scribe Baruch, or a later editor—added this preface on purpose. Jeremiah's call as a "prophet to the nations" (verse 5) makes sense only if we understand that God had a message for the people despite their wrongdoings and that God is in control of all that happens.

Jeremiah's task certainly would not be easy. In Jeremiah 1:19, we read a brief summary of what the prophet's life would be like. Kings, princes, priests, and the populace would fight against him but would not prevail because God would be with the prophet. Thank goodness God followed this dire prediction with words of comfort. Surely Jeremiah needed to hear God's supportive words at the beginning of his ministry! No doubt he would recall them many times as he spoke God's stinging words to the people. As the prophet aroused the opposition of all classes of people, the promise of God's protection must have echoed in his ears. The Bible does not record specific incidents; but the modern reader can be sure that many times Jeremiah reflected on those words of God, "Before I created you in the womb . . ." (verse 5), as he held steadfastly to his faith and as he stood firmly in his call to be God's prophet.

In today's world, Jeremiah serves as a model for those who are willing to make commitments in the face of unpopular opinion. Jeremiah knew he would never win a popularity contest, yet God had called him to a difficult task and Jeremiah committed himself to performing that task. Modern people who feel called by God to pursue a nontraditional career or to work for the solution of an unpopular cause can readily identify with Jeremiah's reluctance. The people who work for improved conditions for the oppressed, whether the oppressed are within the workplace or outside the country, can sense Jeremiah's hesitancy to preach to friends who turn hostile when confronted by the sin of oppression.

Jeremiah 1 has much to say to us today. As we consider what it means to respond to God's call, we need to be careful not to think too narrowly. We often equate being "called" with only professional ministry or mission. This view does a disservice, however, to God and to us. As Christians, we are each called into God's service, and that call may take a variety of forms.

Good News, Bad News

It is into this background that Jeremiah spoke his heartfelt prophecies. In Jeremiah 5, it seems as if a word of grace is coming to Judah despite its sins. Jeremiah speaks of going in search of one person "who acts justly and seeks truth" (verse 1) so that the city might be pardoned.

This is an old concept. We find the same idea in Genesis 18:23-33, in which Abraham argues with God over the destruction of Sodom. Abraham finally gets God to agree to save the city for the sake of ten righteous people, even less than what is demanded of Judah. If Jeremiah can find only one faithful person, even a hint of obedience to the covenant, then the nation will be spared.

Jeremiah built his story's suspense by detailing his search. He looked and looked but could find no such person. Then he realized that he was searching among the poor who perhaps had not been properly educated in God's ways and therefore did not know any better (verse 4). So Jeremiah went to those who were "powerful people" (CEB), "leaders" (New International Version), "rich" (NRSV), or "great" (King James Version), who certainly had been taught God's ways and knew what was required of them (verse 5). The story builds in horror as the prophet searches among the leaders of the land and still can find no one who acts with justice and truth.

Jeremiah goes on to describe the self-imposed destruction of the covenant in startling symbolism: "They too have broken their yoke and shattered the chains" (verse 5). The "yoke" of the covenant, life as servants to God, had been thrown off as if they were untamed animals. The result would be another, far harsher yoke that they could not escape. Part of Jeremiah's horror was that the people so willingly threw off the one when the other loomed so clearly. As the rest of Jeremiah 1–25 proclaims, Babylon would soon arrive as God's instrument against this unrepentant people.

God could not ignore the people's wickedness any longer. They were committing adultery, going to the houses of prostitutes, and "snorting" after one another's wives (verses 7-9). It is unclear whether these verses are meant to be literal or metaphorical. On a literal level, perhaps the people had so abandoned the Ten Commandments that adultery was now commonplace. In addition, the Old Testament often uses a lapse in sexual morals to indicate a lapse of covenant obligations in all respects. On the other hand, adultery is often figurative for going after other gods, and houses of both male and female prostitutes were maintained in the service of certain deities. Perhaps these verses refer to the activities of people engaged in the rites of some of these pagan religions. Either way, it is clear that the people had violated their covenant oath and deserved to be punished. Thus, in Jeremiah 5:10-11, we read that most of Judah and Israel would be stripped away because of their unfaithfulness.

Worst of all, the people had "lied about the LORD" (verse 12). They had predicted that God would do nothing, leaving them unpunished for their sins. They did not expect to see either "war or famine" (verse 12). Moreover, they said, "The prophets are so much wind; the word isn't in them" (verse 13). God's wrath would then come on these scoffers for sure because of their arrogance and ignorance.

To show the people just how wrong they were, God's word would be a fire in Jeremiah's mouth to "consume" the people (verse 14). Jeremiah would tell how God was going to bring a nation from far away to tear down Judah. A frightening image of Babylonia is presented here:

> It is an established nation,
>   an ancient nation,
>   a nation whose language
>   you don't know,
>   whose speech you won't understand.
> Its weapons are deadly;
>   its warriors are many.
>
> (verses 15-16)

The Babylonians would destroy everything. They would eat up the harvest and food, the sons and daughters, the flocks and herds, the vines and fig trees. Nothing that promises life or a future would remain. In an ironic twist, God maintained that "it will shatter your fortified towns in which you trust—with the sword!" (verse 17).

As horrible as this would be, worse was still to come. God would not let the people die. Instead, they would live through this horror and see even more. Because the people had forsaken God and served foreign gods in their land, they would be made to serve strangers in a land that was not theirs (verses 18-19).

Throughout Jeremiah 1–25, the people are described as foolish and senseless. They did not fear God, the same God who set the boundaries on the sea itself. They did not respect or worship God in their hearts, the same God who makes the rain and sets the seasons of the year. Instead, they had chosen stubbornness and rebellion, iniquities and sins. Rather than being children of God, they were a nation of scoundrels and cheats. They grew fat and sleek from the oppression of others. They did not care for the orphan or defend the rights of the needy. They had pushed God to the point where punishment was unavoidable. The horror of the entire situation is summed up here:

> The prophets prophesy falsely,
> the priests rule at their sides,
> and my people love it this way!
> But what will you do when the end comes?
>
> (5:31)

Judah had not respected either God or the prophets, and it had not respected God's covenant conditions. The nation had abandoned justice and truth as a way of life, so God would abandon it to the Babylonians. Judah would learn the hard way that God did indeed care about their attitudes and deeds.

Enough Is Enough!

Jeremiah's concerns are summed up in Chapter 7. Judah had previously been blessed by an opportunity for reform under King Josiah (2 Kings 22), but Jeremiah watched this lead nowhere. If anything, the reform had done more harm than good, giving people the impression that God lived in the Temple and would not allow any harm to come to it. They believed that no consequences would come of their behavior, no matter how unjust or idolatrous, because God had pledged that Jerusalem would stand forever.

About the Scripture

The Queen of Heaven

Jeremiah frequently warned people of the consequences. In Jeremiah 7:16-20, we see an image of entire families engaged in the worship of other deities. Children gather wood for their fathers to make a fire on which their mothers will bake cakes for the "Queen of Heaven." In addition, the whole family pours out drink offerings to other gods. As a result, God would destroy the entire place. All life—human beings, animals, trees, and fruit—would be wiped away. All signs of the fertility of the land, represented by the supposed other deities, would be erased by the one God who is the true creator.

Other ancient Near Eastern texts describe cakes like those mentioned in Jeremiah 7:16. The cakes were often symbolically shaped in honor of some fertility goddess. This tradition may have begun within practices related to the worship of Ishtar, a major Babylonian/Assyrian mother goddess figure. The "Queen of Heaven", unidentified in this text, may refer to her, the West Semitic goddess Astarte, or the Canaanite fertility goddess Asherah.

For Jeremiah, this brick wall of complacency and indifference seemed impenetrable. He tried to warn the people that they would bring destruction on themselves. True, they came to the Temple to "worship." They offered the traditional sacrifices and offerings. Yet the very fact that they came to the Temple as if all was well showed their hypocrisy. Their daily lives went against God's law, so how dare they come to the Temple as if they were righteous?

The rest of the passage presents a dismal picture. God had tried for years to keep the people on a right path. Since the Exodus, the Lord had been sending prophets to teach covenant responsibilities, but the people remained stubborn. They persisted in following their own ways. Now Jeremiah faced a hopeless situation. He would deliver the word of the Lord, but the people would not listen. Because of this, the people themselves would be slaughtered and God would end all happiness in Jerusalem. The land and all within it would become a waste.

Jeremiah's message to the people strikes at the heart of their predicament. The people honestly did not realize that they were doing wrong and that was part of the problem. They would never be able to turn from wrong as long as they could not recognize wrongdoing in the first place. They thought they could appease God by going to the Temple and going through the motions of "right religion." They thought going through the motions of performing sacrifices, burnt offerings, and prayers would be enough for God to think they were doing their duty. They were content to give God the minimum due, believing it was enough to keep God off their backs. They did not understand that God demanded more. God expected obedience, shown through justice to neighbor and worship of

Across the Testaments

Jesus in the Temple

Jeremiah's accusation about the Temple being turned into a "hiding place for criminals" (7:11) echoes in Jesus' accusations against injustice and moneymaking in the temple in Matthew 21:13, Mark 11:17, and Luke 19:46.

God alone. Without this obedience, the rites and rituals of religion meant nothing. In acting out religious ritual not coupled with obedience, the people had managed to turn worship in the Temple into an insult to God. The time had come when God would tolerate this no longer.

Live the Story

As we read Jeremiah's text about a time in Judah's history over twenty-five hundred years ago, it is easy to identify with the prophet. We understand that we are called to confront hypocrisy in others. If we have any problem at all, it is perhaps that we are not always as confrontational as we might be. The reality is that all of us stand in need of God's grace daily. In fact, most of us count on that grace. Indeed, if we did not, how could we go on? If we could not count on God's forgiveness, how could we stand to face another day, knowing that we are doomed to fail at being perfect?

It is much harder to confront hypocrisy in ourselves. If we examine our own lives closely, though, we find that Jeremiah's list may hit closer to home than we like to admit. Most of us go to church on Sunday and feel very good about who we are and how we live, but consider the following: How often have you passed up an opportunity to help someone who is helpless and in need? What efforts, if any, have you taken to address the problems with violence in your community? Do you find that as your life gets busy and "something has to give," it is your prayer time or worship time that is sacrificed? When you go to make a major purchase in your life, do you ask, Is this what God would have me do with this money?

Our challenge and our hope comes in Jeremiah's call to quit hiding behind feel-good religious doctrine and to take honest looks at our lives. We need to be honest about where we fall short of our covenant responsibilities. We need to look at the ways to face the reality of who we are and what we do. If we come before God in honesty, humility, and repentance, then indeed we will have reason to feel good about ourselves and our relationships with our Lord when we join together in worship. Furthermore, we discover that we can take the steps we need to take in order to practice justice, mercy, and care for our neighbors.

6.

Prophecies Against Other Nations

Jeremiah 46–51

Claim Your Story

In the account of the prophet's call in Jeremiah 1, God speaks of the divine power "over nations and empires, to dig up and pull down, to destroy and demolish, to build and plant" (verse 10). In discussing this verse during a Bible study at my church, an impassioned argument once arose over the nature of sin and suffering in the world. One participant, holding fast to the concept of God's sovereignty, maintained that ultimately God must be to blame for all that goes wrong in the world and spoke of how troubling that was to him. Others emphasized human free will, defending God's good nature. The first speaker responded, "As I see it, there are only two choices. Either God is in control or God isn't. How can God be God and not be in control? But if God is in control, why aren't things better? No, I can't see goodness in allowing things to go on as they are."

As we look around the world in general, we continue to wrestle with this question. Each week there are headlines about murdered children, and domestic violence exists within all of our communities. Our neighborhoods are full of foreclosure signs as a result of the bad economy, and family after family is affected by layoffs or reduced salaries. Weather patterns seem to be getting worse, with more natural disasters coming all the time. There seems to be no end to hunger, poverty, and war around the world. So is God in control or not?

About the Christian Faith

Theodicy

Theodicy is the theological term used for the area of inquiry that deals with questions about God's omnipotence and justice in the midst of evil. The word comes from the combination of the Greek words for God (*theos*) and justice (*dikē*) and was first used by Gottfried Wilhelm Leibniz in 1710.

For Jeremiah, the answer was a definite yes. He explained the evils in society as coming from the human heart, and he justified God's actions against the people as the deserved punishment for their sin. Ultimately, however, the prophet pointed to the sovereignty of God as good news. The God who judges is the same God who saves; and this God has the power to save, without a doubt. In fact, this God is so in control of all creation that foreign nations will be used as tools for redemption, whether they like it or not!

Enter the Bible Study

In session 5, we saw how Jeremiah 1–25 lifted up Babylon as the agent of God's judgment against Judah. This theme continues through Jeremiah 45. Chapters 46–51 then shift to judgments against "the nations" (46:1). Taken in order, these are Egypt, Philistia, Moab, Ammon, Edom, Syria (called Damascus), Kedar, Hazor, Elam, and Babylon.

The overall goal of these chapters is to point to God as the indisputable lord of all nations and the whole of creation. We are not always told why these nations are being punished, only that God can and will bring judgment. In the same vein, these chapters are interspersed with promises of God's eventual restoration of Judah.

Oracles Against Egypt

Jeremiah 37:6-10 records how King Zedekiah sought an alliance with Egypt against Babylon despite Jeremiah's protests. Sometime later, other Judeans fled to Egypt, seeking safety after Jerusalem's fall. They took

Jeremiah with them against his will, ignoring his insistence that such a relationship with Egypt was counter to God's will.

The oracles against Egypt begin with a reference to Carchemish, the site of a decisive victory of Babylonia over Egypt in 605 B.C. (46:1-12). The writer maintains that God intended this past defeat, just as God intends the one to come. In language that reminds us of Exodus, the writer describes how God will destroy the Egyptian warriors.

Verses 13-26 contain a second oracle in which the "LORD of heavenly forces" (verse 18) turns Egypt over to Babylon as punishment for pride and bragging (verse 21). Neither Pharaoh nor Apis, the bull god of Egypt, will be able to stand against the Lord.

The section concludes with a strong assurance that, contrary to Egypt, God will save Judah (verses 27-28). Echoing Jeremiah 30:10-11, these verses promise a return to the homeland where the former captives will find "quiet and ease" (46:27; 30:10, NRSV) and the destruction of all nations to which the people were banished (verse 28). Surprisingly, God also intends Egypt's restoration as well (verse 26).

Oracles Against Philistia

The Philistines were some of the Sea Peoples who migrated into the Canaanite coastland from the Aegean area during the twelfth century B.C. Mention of them usually calls to mind the battles fought by Saul and David. Despite the latter's eventual defeat of the Philistine army, these people kept control of the coastland. In the last days of Judah they were no longer a threat, but they were still remembered as an ancient foe.

As in the oracle against Egypt, the coming destruction will be by Babylon, but by the intent of God (Chapter 47). The oracle tells about the destruction of cities in Philistia, but we are not told why they will be destroyed. The point is that God is in control, and the text does not provide additional explanation.

Oracles Against Moab

Moab was one of the smaller nations neighboring Judah. Located across the Jordan River to the east, its history included conflict with both

Israel and Judah. In Jeremiah's lifetime, the Moabites helped Babylon raid Judah (2 Kings 24:2). Jeremiah included them in his prophecy, advising Judah and the surrounding nations not to rebel against Babylon but to bring their necks "under the yoke of the king of Babylon and serve him and his people" (Jeremiah 27:12). Other prophetic and historical books mention Moab, but none go into as much detail as Jeremiah 48. Numbers 21–24 contains strong denunciations against Moab. Parts of Jeremiah 48 echo other prophetic writings, such as the oracles against Moab in Isaiah 15–16 and Ezekiel 25:8-11.

The oracle begins with language we have seen elsewhere in Jeremiah. Moab will experience the consequences of God's judgment in the form of shame, desolation, great destruction, weeping, and anguish (48:1-9). Jeremiah 48:11-13 describes Moab as a ruined or spilled wine. Misplaced confidence in the god Chemosh will lead to shame. Moab also relied on its military might, as verses 14-20 show. No army can stand against God, however. The powerful Moabites are told to head for the rocks and caves (verse 28). This is what will come of their arrogance and boasting (verses 29-30). It is no wonder that the text predicts extreme grief on Moab's part.

The surprising word of grace is that God also laments for Moab. "My heart wails," says the Lord in Jeremiah 48:36. Verses 31-39 describe how God intended good things for Moab and is anguished that they did not come to fruition. Out of grief and love, after their punishment, God will eventually restore Moab (verse 47).

Can you imagine the surprise (and perhaps outrage) these words would bring to Judean captives in exile? The same promise of restoration God gives to them (30:3) is being made to the Moabites! Thus Jeremiah 48:47 emphasizes the biblical theme of God's care for all and anticipates the glorious plan revealed in Revelation 22 for "the healing of the nations" (verse 2).

Oracles Against Other Nations

Several of the other nations who were enemies of Judah at some point during their history are named in Jeremiah 49. These include Ammon and Edom, Damascus, Kedar and Hazor, and Elam.

Ammon (49:1-6) had been in conflict with the Hebrew people for ages (see Genesis 19:30-38; Judges 10-11; 2 Samuel 10). Like Moab, Ammon once helped Babylon attack Judah (2 Kings 24:2) and later was advised against joining Judah in its rebellion against Babylon (Jeremiah 27). As with Moab, Ammon will eventually fall because it is God's will. Neither the people themselves nor their god Milcom will be able to stand against the Lord. This affirmation of God's power would be especially important to those in exile after 587 B.C. because those deported to Babylon wondered if God was really in control after all. This oracle pronounces a hearty yes!

Jeremiah 49:7-22 turns to Edom, a nation whose heritage traces back to Jacob's twin brother Esau (Genesis 25:30; 36). Biblical writers use the animosity between the two brothers to explain the ongoing conflict between their descendants. Passages like Numbers 20:14ff, Judges 11:17-18, and 2 Kings 14:7-10 give us some idea of the troubles that existed between Edom and the Hebrew people. Edom is to be punished and brought down because of its pride and the way it terrorized others (Jeremiah 49:14-16). Now it will become "a wasteland" (verse 17) instead of a high and mighty bully. God will destroy the nation, leaving protection only for the widows and orphans (verse 11).

The mention of Damascus, the capital of Aram or Syria, in Jeremiah 49:23-27 is a surprise because that nation was not a major player in Jeremiah's time. Defeated by the Assyrians in 732 B.C., it had little to do with Israel or Judah after that. It is not mentioned in either Jeremiah 25 or 27 although other nations are. The oracle, which lifts up the common themes of panic, anguish, and destruction, seems to have been included because of the affirmation of God's power. Syria, like the other nations, will fall because it is God's will.

Jeremiah now turns to a new region (49:28-33). Kedar refers to a nomadic people in a remote area in the north portion of the Arabian desert. Jeremiah may even have been referring to a powerful alliance of nomadic Arab tribes. Pulling together several biblical references, we learn that Kedar was the son of Ishmael, Abraham's son by Hagar (Genesis 25:12-13). His Bedouin descendants lived in tents made of black goat hair

(Song of Songs 1:5) and herded camels, sheep, and goats (Isaiah 60:7; Ezekiel 27:21). They were renowned archers (Isaiah 21:16-17).

Hazor here is not the famous city located nine miles north of Israel. Jeremiah apparently means a site or region in the Arabian Desert. Following Isaiah 42:11, some scholars suggest the word here refers to settlements or the "unwalled cities" inhabited by the Kedar. The people of Kedar and Hazor were not traditional enemies of Israel or Judah, nor are specific sins mentioned in regard to them. The most we are told is that they live safely and in security (Jeremiah 49:31), although the reference to "shaven temples" in Jeremiah 49:32 indicates a variance with Jewish law (Leviticus 19:27). Because there was no apparent reason for Babylon to campaign in this area, scholars speculate that these nations were included to show the breadth of God's reach and control.

The final oracle (Jeremiah 49:34-39) is the only one associated with a king of Judah. Set during Zedekiah's reign, it concerns the nation of Elam, noted for its excellent archers (verse 35). The oracle itself is very general and includes threats similar to those that run throughout the Book of Jeremiah. The text makes clear that Elam's future is in God's hands. If some people in Jeremiah's time hoped Elam could defeat Babylon, this oracle may represent a message from the prophet that Judah should not hope or expect to avoid God's plan for them.

Oracles Against Babylon

Up until now, Babylon has been presented as God's agent of punishment against Judah (Chapters 1–35) and the nations (Chapters 46–49). Now we see God's judgment pronounced on that mighty nation itself. Babylon defeated the Egyptians at Carchemish in 605 B.C. and emerged as a dominant power in the region.[1] Jeremiah understood this to be God's will. God chose to use Babylon as a means of punishment during this time, so it was allowed to flourish. Chapters 50–51 shift, though, to the time for Judah's restoration and thus Babylon's necessary fall to Persia. Babylon is about to be held accountable for its deeds, especially for challenging God (50:24) and for arrogance (50:29, 31-32).

Babylon

Babylon was located about fifty-four miles south of modern Baghdad. It spanned the Euphrates River with a stone bridge connecting both sides of the city. The remains of the site cover over three and a half square miles. Under Nebuchadnezzar, the city became the most prominent in Mesopotamia. He built the famous Ishtar Gate, named for a major goddess there.

Captives from Judah were brought to Babylon in 597 B.C. and again in 586 B.C. Jeremiah foresaw the Jewish return from exile and fall of Babylon that occurred under Cyrus the Persian in 539 B.C. Notably, Babylon was to fall again in 331 B.C., this time to Alexander the Great.

Babylon's defeat and Judah's restoration are intimately linked in these chapters where we find them carefully interwoven. As we read through the verses, we move back and forth between these two themes. The god of Babylon, called both Bel and Merduk in Jeremiah 50:2, will now be put to shame as the power of God is revealed. Babylon will be punished for plundering God's heritage (50:11). Perhaps this refers to excess ravages on the land after God allowed it to be taken.

Jeremiah 50:33-34 uses Exodus imagery to describe what God will do. Like Egypt (Exodus 7:14-24; 8:1-7), Babylon has held the people as slaves and refused to let them go. Yet, once God is done, the people will once more know God is their redeemer (Jeremiah 50:34). What a powerful reminder for people in exile! God has not forgotten or forsaken them but, acting as next of kin, will buy them back from bondage. It is a steadfast promise that we find echoed in the mission of Jesus Christ (see Luke 21:28; Romans 3:24; 8:23; Ephesians 1:7, 14; 4:30; Colossians 1:14; Galatians 3:13; 4:55; and so forth). The gods of Babylon may have appeared to have strength, but they are nothing compared to the creator of heaven and earth. God, who controls all, will bring the Medes (here meaning the Persians) to destroy Babylon; and then all will know the truth: that God has been in control all along (51:15-19, repeating 10:12-16).

Once again, God will act to bring order out of chaos (51:34-44). Echoing Psalms 87:4 and 89:10, Babylon is described as a chaotic sea monster that God will defeat (Isaiah 51:9 names this monster *Rahab*). Jeremiah 51:42-44 end the oracle with an image of the watery, primeval waters of Genesis 1:2 and the floodwaters of Genesis 6–8 overwhelming Babylon, defeating its god, and restoring order to the world—an order marked by the restoration of God's people (51:43-53). The final words of the oracle (51:54-58) emphasize again that Babylon ruled under God's allowance and now will fall at God's will. The Lord who rules "over nations and empires" (1:10) controls even mighty Babylon.

The significance of this theological affirmation shows God's power over all nations, no matter how big. Centuries after Jeremiah lived and prophesied, Revelation looked back to Babylon to reassure persecuted Christians that Rome too would be overcome (Revelation 18).

The oracles against the nations can be problematic for us. Are we to yearn for the destruction of others, celebrating their suffering as well as their demise? The lamentations of God inserted into these chapters suggests not. It seems instead that we are to take another message from these texts: God is in control, God has a plan, and God is working things out despite all contrary human activity. These chapters invite us to trust God, even when it seems God is absent or powerless.

Live the Story

After a forty-year ministry of disappointments and frustrations, Jeremiah 46–51 bursts with hope. Beyond the tragedy of his own time, Jeremiah could see a new day coming. God was in control after all, and that good news made all the difference.

As we go through life, that same good news makes a difference to us. Whether we are coping with another horror story in the news or a personal tragedy of our own, we want to know that God is there, that God cares, and that God is at work to bring some form of renewal.

Ironically, in a sort of "which came first: the chicken or the egg" scenario, many Christians work to make the world a better place because they have hope in God's future; and in the process of their efforts, they find that their hope increases. Consider, for example, the ministry of one small, rural parish in Mississippi. Despite the poverty of the area and the many reasons to give up on trying to make a difference, each person in the church, lay and clergy alike, contributes his or her gifts to ministry. Among the programs established and maintained by the congregation are:

- teaming volunteers with lonely people in a nearby nursing home,
- sending needed items to children in Mexico,
- operating a Meals on Wheels program,
- and supporting a community garden to help combat local hunger.

Other ministries include offering to drive people to the doctor, picking up groceries for people, and sitting with kids in an after-school program.

This congregation chooses to act in love and faithfulness because they believe it is their call. As a result, others in the community see the church's actions as a witness to a God who cares; and in this they find hope. It may not yet be hope for a perfect age to come, but it is at least hope for tomorrow—hope that food will be on the table, hope that children will be cared for, hope that one will not be alone. This little church invites us to consider the question, How might we bear witness to the fact that we believe God is in control and that this is good news?

1. From *Understanding the Old Testament* (Anderson, 1986); page 403.

7.

The Fall and Restoration of Jerusalem

Jeremiah 26–45; 52

Claim Your Story

Have you ever been part of an intervention with a family member or friend? If so, you know how tough these interventions are. We start a conversation with someone we love, fearful that it could lead to a break in the relationship, because we can no longer stand silent in the face of his or her self-harm. If our loved one is in denial about having a problem or is otherwise determined to persist in the behavior, odds are the conversation will not go well. The most we can hope for is to lay seeds for a more fruitful conversation in the future.

Such discussions are not made easier by the human tendency to blame others for everything that happens to us. Just think of some of the seemingly unnecessary statements included with various products such as "remove pie from oven using oven mitts" or "avoid placing fingers in fan blades." (Yes, these are actual instructions!) Such warnings do more than presuppose that some buyers might need this advice; they guard against any lawsuits that might come as a result. A look at court dockets today suggests that, as a society, we are more inclined to see ourselves as victims in any situation and less inclined to take responsibility for the consequences of our own decisions and actions.

Such attitudes are similar to those faced by Jeremiah. Love compelled him to speak out against the people's destructive behavior, but they resented what they saw as his negative attitude and his interference. Then as now, people wanted to hear good things about themselves without being called to accountability for their behavior. Perhaps this explains, in part, the popularity of certain television evangelists who practice a feel-good approach to religion today. They promise prosperity and a sense of being special without making any demands upon their audience (except perhaps to support their ministries). It is much easier to listen to them than to preachers who challenge us to examine our hearts for places where we may need to change.

Enter the Bible Study

In this lesson, we turn back to the central chapters of Jeremiah (26–45), which are memoirs of the scribe Baruch and the historical appendix found in Jeremiah 52. These chapters cover a range of events in Jeremiah's lifetime:

- A second Temple sermon (Chapters 26; see also 7:1–8:3)
- Jeremiah's confrontations with other prophets and the use of a yoke as a warning sign (Chapters 27–28)
- Jeremiah's letter to some Babylon exiles (Chapters 29)
- The beautiful "Little Book of Consolation" or "The Scroll of Comfort" (CEB) that speaks of the restored community (Chapters 30–31)
- Jeremiah's symbolic purchase of a field in Anathoth (Chapter 32)
- The promise of healing and restoration that God will accomplish and warnings to King Zedekiah (Chapters 33–34)
- Jeremiah commends the Rechabites (Chapter 35)
- The burning of the prophet's scroll by King Jehoiakim (Chapter 36)
- And Jeremiah's sufferings (Chapters 37–44).
- The fall of Jerusalem (Chapter 39)

The section ends with God's word to Baruch (Chapter 45). Chapter 52 is a review of the destruction of Jerusalem, the deportations, and King Jehoiachin's removal to Babylon. As a means of entering into the themes of these chapters, we will focus on Jeremiah 27–29, 31, and 37.

Disputes Regarding God's Plan

In 598 B.C., Nebuchadnezzar II of Babylon quelled a rebellion in Jerusalem and replaced the current king Jehoiachin (who had only reigned for three months) with his uncle Zedekiah. The first deportation of exiles happened in 597 B.C., although Zedekiah and others were allowed to remain in Judah as vassals. Jeremiah 27:1-4 tells how, in the beginning of Zedekiah's reign, Jeremiah made a yoke of straps and bars to wear upon his neck as a symbol for the long captivity Judah would endure. God also instructed Jeremiah to send word to the kings of Edom, Moab, Ammon, Tyre, and Sidon (27:3) that they would face the same fate one day. Zedekiah was trying to get those nations to join him in rebelling against Babylon, which Jeremiah considered an extremely unwise move, hence the harsh warning to these nations.

That same year, word of Zedekiah's possible rebellion had raised hopes that Judah would regain its freedom and that the exiles soon would return home. Hananiah was one of those who optimistically believed the best. Therefore, he publicly derided Jeremiah for continuing to say the exile would continue. According to Hananiah, God had broken the yoke of Babylon and would return everyone within two years. God would even restore the temple vessels taken by Nebuchadnezzar (28:1-4). Jeremiah disagreed with this assessment, indicating that Hananiah's prophecy was false. In an attempt to regain credibility, Hananiah then broke the yoke Jeremiah wore. Jeremiah went his way and after some time returned with a yoke of iron. Jeremiah then confronted Hananiah and made a grim prophecy: Because Hananiah made the people trust in a lie, he would die within the year. Sure enough, he did.

Jeremiah then sent a letter to the people in exile. Jeremiah 29:1-2 lists some of the people who were in Babylon during the first deportation; the letter mentions elders, priests, prophets, and ordinary people, as well as "King Jeconiah, the queen mother, the court officials, the government leaders of Judah and Jerusalem, and the craftsmen and smiths" (verse 2). The letter encouraged the exiles to establish themselves in Babylon. Jeremiah urged the people to build houses, plant gardens, take wives, have children, and marry off their older children. He told the people to multiply and thrive in captivity. Moreover, he warned them not to listen to false prophets who said they would return home soon. They did not speak in the name of the Lord, Jeremiah said, and would only deceive the people.

God would not restore the people for seventy years (verse 10). Moreover, this was for their own good, to give them "a future filled with hope" (verse 11). Although Jeremiah does not explain the details, he seems to indicate that if the people were to return too soon they might be in danger of losing Judah again in some way. God would act in God's time in order both to restore the people and to guarantee their security. In the meantime, God was with the people and would hear their cries. The promise comes again that God would eventually restore the people to the land.

Jeremiah's letter did not stop there, however. He was honest enough to say that those who remained in the land would suffer. They would be subject to lawlessness, famine, and pestilence until they became an object of derision "an object of horror to all nations on earth and an object of cursing, scorn, shock, and disgrace among all the countries where I have scattered them, because they wouldn't listen to my words, declares the LORD, which I sent them time and again through my servants the prophets. They wouldn't listen, declares the LORD" (verses 18-19). Moreover, the false prophets in Babylon, identified as Ahab and Zedekiah, would die because they spoke false words in God's name (verses 20-23).

Who's Right?

Jeremiah 28–29 raise the issue of who is trustworthy and who is not. When two people each claim to have the truth, how can we distinguish between who is right and who is wrong? The text suggests one answer: only time will tell. Jeremiah himself implied that, after all was said and done, the people would know who was right and who was wrong. Perhaps the truth of Jeremiah's testimony came sooner than expected when Hananiah died as predicted (28:16-17).

The text also implies two other "measures" of a true prophet. First, we see that prophecy often brings an unpopular message. As Jeremiah pointed out, the prophets of Israel usually brought bad news: "The prophets who came before you and me long ago prophesied war, disaster, and disease against many lands and great kingdoms" (verse 8). Jeremiah was proof of this as well. His message was highly unpopular, as we will see.

The second test of a true prophet is a corollary to the first: A true prophet will suffer for the sake of the message, however unpopular. Jeremiah was not happy about the suffering he had to endure, but his persistence in the face of persecution shows how strongly he believed his message to be the word of God. It also shows the lengths to which he was willing to go to serve his Lord. One has to wonder how long Hananiah would have stuck by his opinion if he had to endure the same resistance that Jeremiah faced.

The New Covenant

Prophets in Israel and Judah often reminded the people of their covenant relationship with God, which stretched back through history. The Sinai Covenant, which included the Ten Commandments, lifted up the principles on which the life of the new community was to be based—a new kind of society in which there would be obedience and a willingness to accept responsibility for each other in ways that protected the integrity of relationships.

Across the Testaments

A Covenant Written on the Heart

Christians have treasured Jeremiah 31:31-34 as a prediction of the new covenant that came about through Christ. This prediction even forms the source of the title of the "New Testament"; and in Luke 22:14-20, the language of a new covenant occurs with the thanksgiving over the cup (see 1 Corinthians 11:25 and 2 Corinthians 3:6) and also in Hebrews 8:10-12 and 10:10-18. The language of the new covenant in the last Passover meal shared by Jesus and the disciples points to God's purposes at work in and through Jesus. The text in Hebrews suggests that the first covenant was "obsolete," but that is not what Jeremiah says in 31:31-34. The problem was not with the covenant, but with the people who broke the covenant, which is similar to Paul's view in Romans 7:7-12. Jeremiah wanted to tell people who had almost given up that there was still a reason to hope and that God is our true source of hope. What we recognize with hindsight is that God's hope is always present. It was present in the horrors of the Babylonian destruction of Jerusalem, and it continues for all eternity in Jesus Christ.

The covenant God made with Abraham focused more on God's promises, as did the covenant that threw a wall of protection around the throne of David. People found it easy to become complacent under these two covenants.

When the tragedy of the exile came at last and people saw how terrible the punishment was, they did much soul searching. Why had it all happened? How could they prevent such a terrible thing from happening again? Was there any hope? Some dealt with the burden of guilt by the common human strategy of avoidance. "God is punishing us," they said, "not because of our sin but because of the sins of those who have gone before us." Jeremiah rejects this idea: "In those days they shall no longer say, 'The parents have eaten sour grapes, and the children's teeth are set on edge' " (31:29, NRSV). The prophet Ezekiel wrestled with this idea as well and, like Jeremiah, flatly repudiated the old saying (see Ezekiel 18:1-4). Both place responsibility on the current generation. Jeremiah says that people shall die for their own sin (Jeremiah 31:30).

Even so, hope existed. God still longed for a relationship with the people. Jeremiah 31:31-34 says that God would bring an inner change in people, a spiritual transformation designed to foster covenant faithfulness. Both Judah and Israel would be restored into a new covenant:

> This is the covenant that I will make with the people of Israel after that time, declares the Lord. I will put my Instructions within them and engrave them on their hearts. I will be their God, and they will be my people. They will no longer need to teach each other to say, 'Know the LORD!' because they will all know me, from the least of them to the greatest, declares the LORD; for I will forgive their wrongdoing and never again remember their sins.
>
> (31:33-34)

A Symbol of Hope

When the outlook was most desperate for the nation and for himself, Jeremiah indicated in a dramatic way that there was still hope. The catastrophe was certain, he said, but afterward a time of prosperity and peace would come again. He symbolized this by exercising his right to purchase a piece of land that belonged in the custody of his family (32:6-15). He made the transaction as a symbol of hope for a time when the exile would be over and God would bless a chastened people. At the time, it seemed a strange and foolish investment to buy land that soon would be overrun by enemy troops. However, Jeremiah did so as a way of expressing the message from God that someday homes would be built, children would play, and families would live in peace again in the land. Out of the suffering, hope would come, not as a dream but as a reality. In the fullness of time, God would restore the people and their land where they would be led by a prince who was right with God (30:18-22).

Dire Times

Surely there were times when Jeremiah doubted, even a little, that the new covenant would ever come to pass. He lived in a terrible time, experiencing the pain of seeing clearly the events all around him; so it would be far easier to anticipate the inevitable calamity ahead. Yet for all of his sincerity and the authority of conviction with which he spoke, Jeremiah could not make his fellow citizens see what they did not want to see, good or bad. His warnings were not only ignored, they aroused such hostility that on occasions his life was in danger.

Despite his messages of hope, the people and their leaders could not forgive Jeremiah for holding them to account and prophesying punishment for their sins. Their anger and suspicion led to Jeremiah being arrested for treason (by Hananiah's grandson), and he was subsequently beaten and imprisoned in "a cistern" of an official's home (37:11-16). While he was imprisoned, Zedekiah had Jeremiah brought to him under cover of darkness and asked the beseeching question, "Is there a word from the LORD?" (verse 17). What a picture the story presents! The king trembles, the prophet stands assured, and we wonder who is really the prisoner? The prophet answers with abruptness: "There is!" We can imagine the heavy silence as the king waits with apprehension for the words of doom. The words, when they come, are chilling: "You are going to be handed over to the king of Babylon" (verse 17). Jeremiah then appealed to the king not to send him back to prison, and the king placed him in the care of the military and provided him a daily loaf of bread (verse 21). When Jeremiah continued to pronounce that the city would be handed

About the Scripture

Ebed-Melech

Ebed-melech, the Ethiopian guard who saved Jeremiah from the cistern, is a fascinating character (38:6-13). He heard of the prophet's crisis and acted with compassion. Instead of saying, "I don't want to get involved," he went to the king and alerted Zedekiah to the situation. In turn, Ebed-melech received permission to rescue Jeremiah and then carried his mission to a successful conclusion. The prophet's own countrymen sought to kill him, yet this foreigner living in Jerusalem preserved Jeremiah's life.

over to Babylon, he was thrown into a cistern owned by the king's son. He would have perished quickly had it not been for the compassion of one of the guards (38:6-13).

The sentence was deserved. The behavior of the nation had been shameful for a long time and never worse than in this moment of crisis. For decades the leading citizens had callously disregarded God's law, taking what they could grab for themselves and trampling over others in the process. They even sold their fellow Hebrews into slavery, which was strictly against God's law. The law specified that if a Hebrew citizen was enslaved, he or she had to be set free after six years; this law also had been ignored (34:13-14). Now, a wave of guilt swept over the nation and all the slaves were set free. "Surely," they thought, "God will note this sign of repentance and spare us!" However, they changed their minds and took back the slaves that they had freed (verses 10-11). This dramatic evidence of hypocrisy and greed did not escape the scathing denunciation of the prophet (verses 17-22). It helps explain the earnestness with which he said of the Babylonians, in effect, "They will be back!" (37:6-10).

Live the Story

As Jeremiah knew all too well, the truth hurts. We can all cite examples from life. I am reminded in particular of a young woman who, following a painfully honest discussion, remarked, "I know it's true, otherwise it wouldn't hurt so much." The measure of her maturity was that she was willing to hear the truth despite the pain it caused. The measure of Jeremiah's dedication to God was that he was willing to endure rejection and danger when truth needed to be spoken in love.

As we look back over time to the confrontation between Hananiah and Jeremiah, we find ourselves encountering several difficult questions. How open are we, like the people of Judah, to hearing God's word when it proves difficult? How willing are we, like Jeremiah, to carry an unpopular message to those we love? Even more so, how much are we willing to endure for the sake of that word if we believe it is truly God's own? The answers to these questions are not found in a moment or in a single situation; they emerge as we struggle every day to live the life to which we have been called. Within our efforts, we rejoice that God says to us, as to the Judeans, "Don't be afraid. . . . I am with you" (30:10a, 11a).

What better message could emerge for us when all the world seems to be falling apart, and we are not sure we can trust ourselves to stand fast in doing what's right? In the texts for this lesson, God says, "Accept responsibility for what you do; be accountable for your actions"; and then God continues, "Live out the law that I have written on your hearts, for I choose to be in a covenantal relationship with you." Centuries ago, God spoke these words of encouragement through the prophet Jeremiah at a time when the world looked very bleak. That same word of encouragement is offered to us today.

8.

Mourning for Jerusalem's Holocaust

Lamentations

Claim Your Story

What do you do when your world falls apart? How do you endure? What helps your faith survive? These are some of the questions raised by the Book of Lamentations.

We don't have to be in a church community, or any community, very long before these questions come up. For example, I think of the following stories, all of which occurred during the course of a single year in a moderately sized congregation:

- A professional musician, whose work was his life, lost two fingers in an accident. He wrestled with thoughts of suicide, firmly believing that no joy was left to him. What words of comfort could we offer him?

- A woman who believed she had a perfect marriage discovered that her husband was cheating on her—with her sister. Her world crumbled in learning that the two people whom she loved and trusted the most were not as she thought. How could she ever love or trust again?

- A recently reconciled couple was overjoyed to discover that the wife was pregnant with their third child. Then, on the way home from a doctor's appointment, she and the baby were killed in a car crash along with the couple's young son. How were the father and daughter to get over their loss?

- Another couple that had tried for close to a decade to have a child finally became pregnant only to learn there was a problem. After the child was born, they were told that he would never develop beyond the stage of a six-month-old baby. How were they to cope with their grief over what could have been in the years to come?

There were other stories as well—deaths of parents and spouses, loss of jobs, the foreclosure on a home—but these four were the worst. As the congregation banded together in what seemed like blow after blow, they found themselves sharing stories of God's presence in other dark times. Together they reminded one another of God's care and compassion, and together they got through that horrible year. Their testimony is a fitting backdrop to the songs of Lamentations.

Enter the Bible Story

The fall of Jerusalem was the single greatest tragedy in the life of the covenant community. The people expressed their grief in songs of mourning, some of which have been preserved in the Book of Lamentations.

Lamentations 1 describes Jerusalem in haunting terms. The recurring image is that of a woman abandoned and alone. The use of first-person language (*I* and *me*) enhances the sense of despair. Over and over again we hear Jerusalem speak personally to God about her sorrow and her loss.

Lamentations 2 focuses on God's anger. Verses 1-10 describe how God destroyed Jerusalem in fierce anger without mercy. Everything is now gone that once marked Jerusalem as the holy city of God. Thus, in verses 11-17, the poet speaks a word of personal lament. The poem talks of endless weeping over the sight of starving infants and children dying in their mothers' arms. The poet's grief is increased by the awareness that God tried to warn the people that this would happen.

The poem encourages the people to cry out to God day and night. If they repent, it suggests, God might turn events around and save the city (verses 18-19). The poet then addresses God in Lamentations 2:20-22, begging the Lord to look at the chaos in the city and to consider ending it. Jerusalem has been punished and now enough is enough. The closing words sum up everything: Jerusalem had been the holy city where pilgrims

About the Scripture

Acrostic Poems

The structure of the laments indicates a great deal of thought. The first four are acrostic poems: Each verse begins with a successive letter of the Hebrew alphabet. The fifth psalm carries this theme by having twenty-two verses, thus mirroring the number of letters in the Hebrew alphabet. Acrostic poems were written as a tribute to the subject matter, and few subjects were taken more seriously than the fall of Jerusalem.

came to worship God, but now it is a festival for enemies who are coming to destroy.

Lamentations 3 affirms that God's steadfast love endures. The first twenty verses vividly describe Judah's pain and punishment, but then a shift occurs in verse 21. The poet recalls Scripture verses and other testimonies to God's goodness that gave cause for hope.

The last eleven verses add a rather surprising twist to the end of the lament. Verses 55-60 indicate that to some degree God's salvation has already occurred. The poet (or Judah) has called on God in some way, and God has taken up the cause. Verses 61-66, however, make a surprising request of God: Pay back my enemies!

Lamentations 4 speaks specifically of Zion's punishment. Again we see many of the images of horror described in other texts. Verses 2-4 begin by describing the plight of the young: Infants suffer from thirst, and children beg for food but receive none. The image is of a desperate city where adults are pushed to extremes to survive, even at the expense of children's lives. Perhaps the worst example of all is where the poet says, "The hands of loving women boiled their own children to become their food during the destruction of the daughter of my people" (verse 10). The children are not the only ones to suffer, however. The wealthy now also starve and die in the streets. Those who wore fine clothes find themselves clinging to ash heaps. The ruling class, who were literally among the beautiful people, are now unrecognizable as a result of hunger and suffering. No wonder the poet maintains that Jerusalem's punishment is worse even than Sodom's (verse 6).

The poet's grief over Jerusalem's fall translates over the centuries. We can still hear the emotion in verses 11-15 as the poet describes the way no one, Judeans or otherwise, thought Jerusalem would ever fall. All of the nations of the world believed that Jerusalem was safe because of the power of God. However, now she has been punished for her sins, and the loss is beyond words. The people watched in vain for help to the very end: "From our watchtower we watched for a nation that doesn't save" (verse 17). Egypt had come to their aid once before but not this time. The Babylonians had already defeated Egypt. Lamentations 4:18-20 then describes how the people tried to escape once the city had fallen. They ran into the mountains and the wilderness, but they were pursued by the Babylonians who were "faster than airborne eagles" (verse 19). Many were captured and taken into captivity, including the king, the one under whom they expected to live indefinitely (verse 20). The unbelievable had happened.

When All Is Lost

The closing lament highlights the people's sorrow and repentance. It ends on a qualified word of hope that God will save the people and restore them, unless they have perhaps pushed God beyond the point of no return. The people have good reason to grieve. They have lost every bit of security they once had. They had taken for granted every aspect of life, but they were now gone.

"Our property has been turned over to strangers; our houses belong to foreigners" (5:2). Anyone who has been robbed knows what it is like to have a stranger in one's home. It is an odd, unsettling feeling to know that a stranger has been through your belongings, searching through the intimate places of your own home. For the Judeans, this sense of invasion into one's most private and precious place was even worse—strangers actually lived in their homes.

The loss of home was possibly more devastating for these ancient covenant people than for us. The land was their inheritance in both a legal and spiritual sense. The land had been given to them by God as a place where they would live forever in covenant relationship with their creator and with one another. Now the land itself, and the covenant relationship it symbolized, was "turned over" to others.

"We have become orphans, having no father; our mothers are like widows" (verse 3). This imagery is yet another way to describe the impact of the loss of Jerusalem and Judah. Then, as now, children counted on their parents to provide financial, spiritual, and emotional stability. In the ancient Near East, in particular, the father was critical in each of these areas. The father usually provided the family's sole income, and he also served as the primary teacher of religious values. Without him, the family suffered economically and religiously. Thus the experience of exile is compared to losing a father; God would no longer act as the people's provider, teacher, and loving parent. As a result, their future was uncertain, and they must face it alone. There was no one to guide them, no one to help them. Their struggle for survival would be without comfort because all connection to their God was lost.

"We drink our own water—but for a price; we gather our own wood—but pay for it" (verse 4). Even the basics of life came at a cost. Water was necessary for human survival and also for the survival of the animals and plants that provide humans with food. Wood was necessary for cooking, heat, and certain basic shelter. These former gifts of God, once provided by the land, had been reduced to items to be purchased.

"We get our bread at the risk of our lives because of the desert heat" (verse 9). The fundamental structure of society had been lost. The community had become so lawless and chaotic that people must risk their lives in order to seek bread to survive. All sense of comfort and security had been stripped away. "Our skin is as hot as an oven because of the burning heat of famine" (verse 10). God had given the people a land that was "full of milk and honey" (Numbers 13:27). At this point, however, the people were cut off from all the blessings of the land and left to starve.

Remember, O Lord

In the face of all this loss, Lamentations 5 begins with a call to God to remember them. Remembrance is a significant theme throughout the Old Testament and is a major covenant term. Its use here is full of theological

Across the Testaments

Remembering

Remembering is a key idea in Christian tradition. In the words of institution said at every enactment of the Lord's Supper (1 Corinthians 11:23-26), we too speak of remembering. We take the bread and cup because Jesus told us to do so "to remember me" (verse 25). The reason is both simple and profound: "Every time you eat this bread and drink this cup, you broadcast the death of the Lord until he comes" (verse 26). We remember the disgrace of Jesus' shameful death as a criminal upon the cross. We also proclaim this same death as an opportunity for God's saving power to act in the world as never before. We remember the death of Jesus in order to remember the grace of God, which shows that God remembered us and acted on our behalf.

significance. In most Old Testament writings, remembrance is intimately linked with covenant. For example, after the flood, God creates the rainbow and places it in the sky as a sign. God then states that whenever the rainbow is seen again in rain clouds, "I will remember the covenant between me and you and every living being among all the creatures. Floodwaters will never again destroy all creatures" (Genesis 9:15). Likewise, when the people were enslaved in Egypt, "God heard their cry of grief, and God remembered his covenant with Abraham, Isaac, and Jacob" (Exodus 2:24). The Old Testament records many other incidents throughout the life of the covenant people where God remembered and acted on the covenant promises.

We should note that here in Lamentations 5, God is asked to remember the people's disgrace (verse 1). By remembering the disgrace, God will mark it, giving it significance. Their shame will gain meaning if it becomes part of God's memory. Moreover, the people are asking God to pay attention to what has happened to them and to act in grace to overturn it. The request for God to "remember" is a prayer for God to bring about redemption.

There is little hope expressed in Lamentations 5, no assurance that God would act to save the people. Nonetheless, the people were sure that God could act. The power to save was there, and this reality provided what little hope they had.

How Far Is Too Far?

The heart of this lament is much more than the fall of Jerusalem or the desperate living conditions faced by those who remained behind; it is the sense of being abandoned by God. Judah had fallen. Jerusalem and the Temple were no more. No wonder the writer laments, "Joy has left our heart; our dancing has changed into lamentation" (5:15). With an end to the Davidic monarchy and to the Temple itself, the people must have felt completely cut off from their God. Nonetheless, the writer affirms that God had not abandoned them. God was still God, the one who reigns forever and whose "throne lasts from one generation to the next" (verse 19). God remains sovereign despite the tragedy of the people.

For the people, however, everything had changed. The poet cries out in the voice of the multitude, "Why do you abandon us for such a long time?" (verse 20). The greatest tragedy of all was that God had apparently forgotten the people; if only God would remember them, there might be hope. This is the hope behind the prayer in Lamentations 5:21—that God would remember the people and the covenant. Imagine all the voices of those in the congregation that remained in Jerusalem joining together and saying, "Return us, LORD, to yourself. Please let us return! Give us new days, like those long ago" (verse 21). At last the people had learned their lesson. They must first be restored to God before any other healing could take place. Once they were restored in relationship to the Creator, then all else would be restored as well. They would be renewed and all would be as it was. Until they were right with God, however, nothing else would be right for them.

Unless. What a frightful word this must have been on the lips of the congregation! "Unless you have completely rejected us, or have become too angry with us" (verse 22). The writer and the worshipers who repeated these words recognized that perhaps they finally had pushed God too far. Perhaps their stubborn refusal to return to God and the covenant life had persisted for so long that there truly was no hope of restoration. Worst of all, if this was true, they had no one to blame but themselves. If this was God's final judgment, then it was only what the people deserved.

This raises an interesting theological question for us. Can we truly push God too far? Can we push God to a point beyond which the divine grace won't occur? The basic answer to this is no. There is no sin so great or terrible that God cannot forgive it. There is no human force on earth more powerful than God's grace. Few words have expressed this better than those of the apostle Paul:

> I'm convinced that nothing can separate us from God's love in Christ Jesus our Lord: not death or life, not angels or rulers, not present things or future things, not powers or height or depth, or any other thing that is created.
> (Romans 8:38-39)

Of course, we may choose not to seek or accept such grace, but that does not diminish God's willingness to forgive. In the words of a psalmist, "But you, my Lord, are a God of compassion and mercy; you are very patient and full of faithful love" (Psalm 86:15). Thanks be to God!

Live the Story

Few of us have experienced a communal tragedy like the destruction of Jerusalem, yet many of us know what it is like to suffer a significant loss. Every congregation has someone who has experienced the death of a loved one; and most congregations have members who have survived divorce, financial ruin, or severe physical trauma.

We know through personal experience or through the lives of those close to us what it is like to face an apparently overwhelming tragedy. Such events unfortunately are a part of life. How is it, then, that life goes on? How do we, like those sent into exile so many years ago, find the strength, the courage, and the sheer willpower to go on?

Psychologists speak of stages of grief through which we move back into a wholeness of being. As human beings, these are part of our psychological makeup; and under normal conditions they form our emotional healing process. As Christians, we have another answer as well. We persevere because we have hope. We trust that Jesus Christ, who overcame sin and death, will overcome our difficulties and our sorrows in the proper

About the Christian Faith

Devastated Cities

One commentator, Richard D. Nelson, helps bring home the sense of loss and shock when he writes, "The smoking ruins of Jerusalem are not hard for us to recreate in our imaginations. The devastated city could well be the symbol of our age: Warsaw and Berlin, Dresden and Stalingrad, Hiroshima and Nagasaki. We can trace the contribution to such horrors made by the sin and folly of our contemporary Jehoiakims and Zedekiahs. Whether we also have the theological vision to see in them the hand of God is another matter."[1]

time. After all, Jesus taught that God loves us and is with us in the midst of any suffering, working to bring us back into the fullness of life. Paul, writing about the realities of living as human beings in the world, put it this way: "But we have this treasure in clay pots so that the awesome power belongs to God and doesn't come from us. We are experiencing all kinds of trouble, but we aren't crushed. We are confused, but we aren't depressed. We are harassed, but we aren't abandoned. We are knocked down, but we aren't knocked out. We always carry Jesus' death around in our bodies so that Jesus' life can also be seen in our bodies" (2 Corinthians 4:7-10).

1. From *First and Second Kings*, by Richard D. Nelson, Interpretation (John Knox Press, 1987), p. 265.

Leader Guide

People often view the Bible as a maze of obscure people, places, and events from centuries ago and struggle to relate it to their daily lives. IMMERSION invites us to experience the Bible as a record of God's loving revelation to humankind. These studies recognize our emotional, spiritual, and intellectual needs and welcome us into the Bible story and into deeper faith.

As leader of an IMMERSION group, you will help participants to encounter the Word of God and the God of the Word that will lead to new creation in Christ. You do not have to be an expert to lead; in fact, you will participate with your group in listening to and applying God's life-transforming Word to your lives. You and your group will explore the building blocks of the Christian faith through key stories, people, ideas, and teachings in every book of the Bible. You will also explore the bridges and points of connection between the Old and New Testaments.

Choosing and Using the Bible

The central goal of IMMERSION is engaging the members of your group with the Bible in a way that informs their minds, forms their hearts, and transforms the way they live out their Christian faith. Participants will need this study book and a Bible. IMMERSION is an excellent accompaniment to the Common English Bible (CEB). It shares with the CEB four common aims: clarity of language, faith in the Bible's power to transform lives, the emotional expectation that people will find the love of God, and the rational expectation that people will find the knowledge of God.

Other recommended study Bibles include *The New Interpreter's Study Bible* (NRSV), *The New Oxford Annotated Study Bible* (NRSV), *The HarperCollins Study Bible* (NRSV), the *NIV and TNIV Study Bibles*, and the *Archaeological Study Bible* (NIV). Encourage participants to use more than one translation. *The Message: The Bible in Contemporary Language* is a modern paraphrase of the Bible, based on the original languages. Eugene H. Peterson has created a masterful presentation of the Scripture text, which is best used alongside rather than in place of the CEB or another primary English translation.

One of the most reliable interpreters of the Bible's meaning is the Bible itself. Invite participants first of all to allow Scripture to have its say. Pay attention to context. Ask questions of the text. Read every passage with curiosity, always seeking to answer the basic Who? What? Where? When? and Why? questions.

Bible study groups should also have handy essential reference resources in case someone wants more information or needs clarification on specific words, terms, concepts, places, or people mentioned in the Bible. A Bible dictionary, Bible atlas, concordance, and one-volume Bible commentary together make for a good, basic reference library.

The Leader's Role

An effective leader prepares ahead. This leader guide provides easy-to-follow, step-by-step suggestions for leading a group. The key task of the leader is to guide discussion and activities that will engage heart and head and will invite faith development. Discussion questions are included, and you may want to add questions posed by you or your group. Here are suggestions for helping your group engage Scripture:

State questions clearly and simply.

Ask questions that move Bible truths from "outside" (dealing with concepts, ideas, or information about a passage) to "inside" (relating to the experiences, hopes, and dreams of the participants).

Work for variety in your questions, including compare and contrast, information recall, motivation, connections, speculation, and evaluation.

Avoid questions that call for yes-or-no responses or answers that are obvious.

Don't be afraid of silence during a discussion. It often yields especially thoughtful comments.

Test questions before using them by attempting to answer them yourself.

When leading a discussion, pay attention to the mood of your group by "listening" with your eyes as well as your ears.

Guidelines for the Group

IMMERSION is designed to promote full engagement with the Bible for the purpose of growing faith and building up Christian community. While much can be gained from individual reading, a group Bible study offers an ideal setting in which to achieve these aims. Encourage participants to bring their Bibles and read from Scripture during the session. Invite participants to consider the following guidelines as they participate in the group:

Respect differences of interpretation and understanding.

Support one another with Christian kindness, compassion, and courtesy.

Listen to others with the goal of understanding rather than agreeing or disagreeing.

Celebrate the opportunity to grow in faith through Bible study.

Approach the Bible as a dialogue partner, open to the possibility of being challenged or changed by God's Word.

Recognize that each person brings unique and valuable life experiences to the group and is an important part of the community.

Reflect theologically; that is, be attentive to three basic questions: What does this say about God? What does this say about me/us? What does this say about the relationship between God and me/us?

Commit to a lived faith response in light of insights you gain from the Bible. In other words, what changes in attitudes (how you believe) or actions (how you behave) are called for by God's Word?

Group Sessions

The group sessions, like the chapters themselves, are built around three sections: "Claim Your Story," "Enter the Bible Story," and "Live the Story." Sessions are designed to move participants from an awareness of their own life story, issues, needs, and experiences into an encounter and dialogue with the story of Scripture and to make decisions integrating their personal stories and the Bible's story.

The session plans in the following pages will provide questions and activities to help your group focus on the particular content of each chapter. In addition to questions and activities, the plans will include chapter title, Scripture, and faith focus.

Here are things to keep in mind for all the sessions:

Prepare Ahead

Study the Scripture, comparing different translations and perhaps a paraphrase.

Read the chapter and consider what it says about your life and the Scripture.

Gather materials such as large sheets of paper or a markerboard with markers.

Prepare the learning area. Write the faith focus for all to see.

Welcome Participants

Invite participants to greet one another.

Tell them to find one or two people and talk about the faith focus.

Ask: What words stand out for you? Why?

Guide the Session

Look together at "Claim Your Story." Ask participants to give their reactions to the stories and examples given in each chapter. Use questions from the session plan to elicit comments based on personal experiences and insights.

Ask participants to open their Bibles and "Enter the Bible Story." For each portion of Scripture, use questions from the session plan to help participants gain insight into the text and relate it to issues in their own lives.

Step through the activity or questions posed in "Live the Story." Encourage participants to embrace what they have learned and to apply it in their daily lives.

Invite participants to offer their responses or insights about the boxed material in "Across the Testaments," "About the Scripture," and "About the Christian Faith."

Close the Session
Encourage participants to read the following week's Scripture and chapter before the next session.
Offer a closing prayer.

1. Prophecies of Judgment Against the Nations
Isaiah 1–10; 13–23; 28–31; 36–39

Faith Focus
We are called to trust in God, to practice God's ways of justice and mercy, and to extend our love into the whole world. To neglect this call places the world and us in peril.

Before the Session
Pray for God's guidance during your time of preparation, and pray for the participants in your Immersion Bible study group. Read the Scriptures for Session 1 and jot down any questions or insights that emerge for you. Consider what questions might emerge from your group. Read Chapter 1 in the study book. Before the participants arrive, write the Faith Focus on a markerboard or a large sheet of paper for all to see. Write the word *Saints* on a markerboard. Have paper and markers on hand for participants.

Claim Your Story
Invite participants to consider words, phrases, or images suggested by the word *saints*. Have them write or draw these on the markerboard beneath the word *saints*. Read or review highlights of "Claim Your Story." Ask: Who are the "saints" in your life? Why? What feelings or thoughts do you have as you consider yourself as a "saint"? What challenges you in this idea?

Enter the Bible Story
Discuss Isaiah 1

Have the group form two teams. Tell both teams to read Isaiah 1. Team One will discuss ways the chapter talks about God's judgment. Team Two will identify ways the chapter talks about hope. Have the teams report the highlights of their discussions with the entire group. Review highlights of the opening section in "Enter the Bible Story" and " A Prophetic Sampler." Ask: What does this chapter say to you about God? What does it say to you about human beings? How do you think it speaks to contemporary human experience?

Identify Words, Phrases, or Images in Isaiah 6:1-13

Read or review highlights of "Isaiah of Jerusalem," "Speaking for God," and "Problems of the Times." Have the group form teams of two or three. Give each team paper and markers. Tell them to read Isaiah 6:1-13 and draw or write about the image that stands out most for them in the Scripture passage. Have them discuss the following questions: What inspires you about this account? What challenges you or makes you curious? What does it say to you about God? about Isaiah? about human beings? about issues related to justice and mercy? Invite the teams to tell about what they drew or wrote and to share highlights of their discussion with the entire group.

Consider Historical Events

Review highlights of the sections "A National Crisis" and "God's Broken Heart." Ask: How does the crisis during Isaiah's time compare to the contemporary situation among nations in our world? Review highlights of Isaiah 7. Ask: What advice does Isaiah offer to Ahaz? What challenges you about his advice? How does Isaiah understand the role of God in this national crisis involving Assyria, Syria, Israel, and Judah? What does this account say to you about right relationship with God? about human arrogance, injustice, and insecurity? about trusting God?

Reflect on the Sign of Immanuel

Read aloud Isaiah 7:10-17. Review the information about the sign of Immanuel in the box "Across the Testaments." Ask: What does the Scripture say about Immanuel? What is the historical context? Why do you think Christians traditionally interpret Isaiah's sign as a way to understand Jesus Christ? What does it say about salvation? about God's active presence and power in our world?

Discuss Judgment and Hope

Review highlights of "A Word of Hope." Ask: What connections do you see between the themes of judgment and hope in Isaiah? What feelings do you have about the prophetic understanding of God's judgment and God's promise of salvation? Read aloud Psalm 46. Ask: How do you see God's presence and power when times are difficult? In what ways does God's presence and power inspire you to live according to God's ways of justice and mercy?

Live the Story

Read the Faith Focus aloud. Review the material in "Live the Story." Ask: What, if anything, would you change or add to the words and phrases about saints we created at the beginning of the session? Read aloud the questions in the closing paragraph, pausing after each question. Have participants prayerfully consider their personal responses to the questions. Invite them to write one response they can make during the week ahead. Close the session with The Lord's Prayer.

2. Prophecies in Favor of Israel
Isaiah 11–12; 24–27; 32–35

Faith Focus

While it is important to recognize the serious consequences of our individual and corporate sin, the message of Isaiah includes hope and promise. Repentance leads to the experience of God's unfailing grace and steadfast love.

Before the Session

Pray for God's guidance during your time of preparation and pray for the participants in your Immersion Bible study group. Read the Scriptures for Session 2 and jot down any questions or insights that emerge for you. Consider what questions might emerge from your group. Read Chapter 2. Before the participants arrive, write the Faith Focus on a markerboard or a large sheet of paper for all to see. Have a large sheet of paper or a posterboard and markers available. Bring a small mirror to the session for the closing activity.

Claim Your Story

Read or review highlights of "Claim Your Story." Ask: How would you respond to the questions raised in this section? Where in our contemporary world do you see the need to establish justice? How do you think Christians can make a difference as individuals and as communities of faith?

Enter the Bible Story

Create Drawings

Have the group form two teams. Assign Isaiah 25:6-8 to Team One and Isaiah 32:16-18 to Team Two. Give each team a large sheet of paper or posterboard and some markers. Have the teams create a drawing that illustrates their assigned Scripture. Tell them to talk about images from contemporary life that would illustrate the Scripture. Invite the teams to tell about their drawings and to share highlights of their discussion with the entire group.

Discuss Isaiah 11 and 12

Tell the participants to form teams of two or three. Have them read Isaiah 11 and 12 and the section "Starting Over" in the study book. Tell them to discuss the following questions: How do these images of a righteous king speak to you? What thoughts or feelings do they evoke for you? Do they seem attainable to you? Why or why not? How might they have offered hope to the people of Judah during a tumultuous time? How might they offer hope to our world today? How do they inspire or challenge you in your relationship with God and with our world? Why do you think Christians find deep meaning in these chapters as a way to understand God's work through Jesus Christ?

Talk About Destruction and New Creation

Read aloud the opening paragraph of "A Cosmic Event." Review highlights of the material in this section. Remind the group that images of large-scale destruction would be familiar to people living during the time of Isaiah the prophet because of the Syro-Ephraimitic war and the ongoing threats from Assyria. Ask: Where in our world today do you think such images speak to daily reality? In the midst of such devastating images of destruction, how do you think people find hope? Where have you seen new creation emerge from destruction and devastation? How do you think God was present? What does the depiction of destruction and new creation say to you about Isaiah's understanding of God's power?

Have Team Discussions of Isaiah 32–35

Read aloud the opening two paragraphs in "Threats and Promises." Have the group form four teams. Assign a chapter to each team as follows: Team One—Chapter 32; Team Two—Chapter 33; Team Three—Chapter 34; Team Four—Chapter 35. Tell the teams to read their chapter and any information about it in the section "Threats and Promises." Have them discuss the following questions about their assigned Scripture: How does it challenge those who first heard the prophecy? How does it challenge us? What does it say to you about God? What does it say to you about humans? How does it offer hope?

Live the Story

Read aloud the Faith Focus and the last two paragraphs of "Live the Story." Have participants pass around a small hand mirror. Tell them to reflect silently and prayerfully on how they would respond to the questions in this section as they look into the mirror. If anyone wants to talk about their responses, invite them to do so. Do not, however, pressure anyone to share. Encourage everyone to find one way in the week ahead that they can move forward in their relationship with God and with the world. Ask: How might you become part of God's promise of hope and new creation? Close the session by reading aloud the Prayer of Saint Francis of Assisi included in this chapter (page 27).

3. Prophecies of Israel's Deliverance
Isaiah 40–48; 58–66

Faith Focus
Even when circumstances are difficult, we can trust God's promise to be with us and to renew us. We look forward to transformation and new life.

Before the Session
Pray for God's guidance during your time of preparation and pray for the participants in your Immersion Bible study group. Read the Scriptures for Session 3 and jot down any questions or insights that emerge for you. Consider what questions might emerge from your group. Read Chapter 3. Before the participants arrive, write the Faith Focus on a markerboard or a large sheet of paper for all to see. Make sure that every participant has access to a Bible for the group reading. Make sure the Bibles used for the reading are all the same translation.

Claim Your Story
Read aloud the Faith Focus and the opening quotes in "Claim Your Story." Ask: What quotes have you heard or relied upon during your hard times? What things have you relied upon to help you or to comfort you during dark nights or troubled times?

Enter the Bible Story
Reflect on "A Timely Message"
Review highlights of "A Timely Message." Ask: What circumstances in your life, if any, have caused you to doubt God's presence and power? What was it like? What does the word *comfort* suggest to you? What images come to your mind when you hear the word? Isaiah uses the image of a shepherd to express God's care and protection. What images best express this for you?

Do a Group Reading
Review highlights of "Let the Journey Begin." Do a group reading of Isaiah 40 as follows. Have the participants form a circle. One person in the circle will begin reading aloud starting at verse 1. They will read a few lines and then randomly stop. The next person will pick up the reading and also randomly stop. Continue this process for reading the chapter until the group has read all of it. After the reading, ask: What words or phrases stand out for you? Why? What do they say to you about God? What do they say to you about God's care for human beings? What do they say to you about God's presence and power? How do you think they offer hope during hard times?

Discuss "Disappointed Expectations"

Review highlights of "Disappointed Expectations." Invite participants to form two teams. One team will be the exiles in Babylon. The other team will be those who remained behind in Judah. Ask the teams to discuss what feelings or thoughts they think their assigned group of Judeans might have about the return of the exiled people after over fifty years. What would it be like for those who continued to live in Judah? For those who lived in Babylon? What tensions might emerge? What situations in your life have been marked by disappointed expectations? Have the teams share highlights of their discussions with the reassembled group.

Discuss Isaiah 65:17-29

Review highlights of "Worth Waiting For" and "Home at Last." Read aloud Isaiah 65:17-29. Ask: What do these images say to you about God's ongoing work of creation in our world? What is most hopeful to you? What challenges you about the images? Why? How do they address circumstances in our world today?

Live the Story

Review "Live the Story." Recall the images of comfort talked about earlier in the session. Invite participants to prayerfully and silently think about ways they can offer comfort to others in their lives during the week ahead. As a closing prayer, read aloud Isaiah 40:1, 31.

4. Prophecies of the Messiah
Isaiah 49–57

Faith Focus

Christians find reassurance in knowing our own punishment has been borne by another, but we also seek understanding in relation to the suffering we find in life. We live in hope and trust in God's power to transform us and the world even through suffering.

Before the Session

Pray for God's guidance during your time of preparation, and pray for the participants in your Immersion Bible study group. Read the Scriptures for Session 4 and jot down any questions or insights that emerge for you. Consider what questions might emerge from your group. Read Chapter 4. Before the participants arrive, write the Faith Focus on a markerboard or a large sheet of paper for all to see. Prepare three graffiti sheets by writing one of the following Scriptures at the top of each of three large sheets of paper or posterboard: 49:1-6; 50:4-9; and 52:13–53:12. Post these sheets in a location such as a wall or a tabletop that is easily accessible to everyone. Have markers available.

Claim Your Story

Read aloud the Faith Focus. Invite a participant to read aloud Isaiah 9:6. Ask: How do the names that Christians associate with Jesus Christ speak to you? Which one means most to you? Why? Have another participant read aloud Isaiah 53:5, 7. Ask: How do you respond to the idea that someone takes your punishment or suffers for you? How does the idea of suffering connect or disconnect from Isaiah 9:6? Explain.

Enter the Bible Story

Create Graffiti Sheets

Point out the graffiti sheets with the Scripture passages from Isaiah that you have posted. Tell the group that these Scriptures are known as the Servant Songs. Review highlights from the opening section of "Enter the Bible Story." Invite participants to write words or phrases or to draw images of ideas that particularly stand out for them as the group explores these passages. Tell them to do this throughout the session as they feel moved to do so. The group will review the graffiti sheets later in the session.

Explore "A Light to the Nations"

Invite a participant to read aloud Isaiah 49:1-6. Review highlights of "A Light to the Nations."

Ask: What does the Scripture say to you about God? about God's expectations for the servant? about the ways God calls human beings today? Ask participants to write or draw on the graffiti sheet for Isaiah 49:1-6 about any words or phrases that stand out for them.

Explore "A Teacher Who Trusts God"

Invite a participant to read aloud Isaiah 50:4-11. Review highlights of "A Teacher Who Trusts God." Ask: What does the Scripture say to you the servant's understanding of suffering? about the servant's understanding of God? about God's expectations for the servant? about God's expectations for us? about strength and power during times of suffering? Ask participants to write or draw on the graffiti sheet for Isaiah 50:4-11 about any words or phrases that stand out for them.

Explore "The One Who Suffers"

Invite a participant to read aloud Isaiah 52:13–53:12. You may want to divide the Scripture into segments and have several participants read aloud. Review highlights of "The One Who Suffers." Ask: What does the Scripture say to you about the servant's understanding of suffering? about the servant's understanding of God? about God's use of suffering in order to restore or save? about suffering on behalf of others? about the suffering of those who are innocent? about strength and power during times of suffering? Ask participants to write or draw on the graffiti sheet for Isaiah 52:13–53:12 about any words or phrases that stand out for them.

Reflect on God's Power to Transform Suffering

Review highlights of "A Transformed Community." Invite participants to offer responses to these questions raised by the writer: What would happen if the covenant community really lived up to its calling to be the servant of God in the world? What if, like the servant, those in exile were able in faith to leave everything in God's hands? What witness and message might that bring to the world? Review highlights of "The Message for Today." Ask: How would you respond to the questions in terms of the contemporary world?

Live the Story

Review highlights of "Live the Story." Invite participants to tell about what they wrote or drew on the graffiti sheets. Invite participants to pray silently about one way they can witness with either words or actions about God's power to transform suffering in our world.

5. Jeremiah's Call and His Warnings to Judah

Jeremiah 1–25

Faith Focus

Our challenge and our hope comes in Jeremiah's call to take honest looks at our lives in order to determine we fall short of our covenant responsibilities. God's grace empowers us to make changes that will help us practice God's ways of mercy, justice, and care for our neighbors.

Before the Session

Pray for God's guidance during your time of preparation, and pray for the participants in your Immersion Bible study group. Read the Scriptures for Session 5 and jot down any questions or insights that emerge for you. Consider what questions might emerge from your group. Read Chapter 5. Before the participants arrive, write the Faith Focus on a markerboard or a large sheet of paper for all to see. To prepare for the "Live the Story" activity, write the words *Challenges* and *Hopes* on a sheet of poster paper or on a markerboard allowing room beneath each word to make a list.

Claim Your Story

Read the Faith Focus aloud. Review highlights of "Claim Your Story." Ask: Who are the "Jeremiahs" in your life? What do they do that makes you think of them as "Jeremiahs"?

Enter the Bible Story

Discuss Jeremiah's Call

Have participants form teams of two or three. Tell them to read Jeremiah 1 and discuss the following questions: What stands out for you? What words, phrases, or images speak most to you? Why? Invite the teams to share highlights of their discussion with the entire group. Review highlights of "The Call and the Promise." Ask: What comes to your mind when you think about God's call to people today? What thoughts do you have about the idea that God calls everyone? How do you respond to the promise that the God who calls us will be with us as we respond? Do you see a word of hope in this chapter? If so, what is it?

Consider Jeremiah's Criticisms

Again, have participants work in teams of two or three. Ask them to read Jeremiah 5 and review highlights of "Good News, Bad News." Tell them to list the primary criticisms against the people of Judah. Tell them to discuss the following questions: How do you respond to Jeremiah's criticisms? What feelings or thoughts do you have about the theological view of being "devoured" by a strange nation as punishment for breaking God's covenant? What relationship do you see between Jeremiah's criticisms of Judah and life in our contemporary world? Do you see a word of hope in this chapter? If so, what is it? Have the teams share highlights of their discussions with the entire group.

Reflect on Worship and Life

Again, have participants work in teams of two or three. Ask them to read Jeremiah 7 and review highlights of "Enough is Enough!" Have the teams discuss the following questions: What feelings or thoughts do you have about Jeremiah's description of the disconnection between worship in the Temple and daily life? In what ways, if any, do Jeremiah's descriptions echo our own lives of faith? What can we learn from Jeremiah about living our faith day by day? Do you see a word of hope in this chapter? If so, what is it? Have the teams share highlights of their discussions with the entire group.

Live the Story

Review highlights of "Live the Story." Read aloud the Faith Focus. Invite everyone to name the challenges and hopes they found in the earlier discussions of the chapters in Jeremiah. List these on the poster paper or markerboard beneath the appropriate word. Invite the participants to pray silently about the ways they feel called to live out their relationship with God. Close the time of silent prayer by reading aloud these words from Jeremiah 7: "If you truly amend your ways and your doings, if you truly act justly one with another, if you do not oppress the alien, the orphan, and the widow, or shed innocent blood in this place, and if you do not go after other gods to your own hurt, then I will dwell with you in this place" (verses 5-7).

6. Prophecies Against Other Nations
Jeremiah 46–51

Faith Focus

Even in the midst of horror or tragedy, we want to know that God cares and that God is at work to bring renewal. We demonstrate God's hope and renewal as we practice mercy, justice, and compassion in all our relationships with others and with our world.

Before the Session

Pray for God's guidance during your time of preparation, and pray for the participants in your Immersion Bible study group. Read the Scriptures for Session 6 and jot down any questions or insights that emerge for you. Consider what questions might emerge from your group. Read Chapter 6. Before the participants arrive, write the Faith Focus on a markerboard or a large sheet of paper for all to see. If possible, locate a Bible map of the time of the fall of Judah. You can find such maps online, in a study Bible, or in an atlas of Bible maps. Collect several recent newspapers or news magazines that feature international stories.

Claim Your Story

Read aloud the section "Claim Your Story." Ask: With whom do you identify most in the writer's Sunday school class? Why? Have you ever had questions about why God allows bad things to happen? How do you answer such questions? What thoughts or feelings do you have about God's power?

Enter the Bible Story
Explore Bible Maps

Read aloud the opening section of "Enter the Bible Story." Invite participants to look at a Bible map and to locate the places mentioned in this section. Ask: What thoughts come to you as you see these locations on the map?

Have Team Discussions

Ask the group to form six teams. Assign each team one of the following chapters: Jeremiah 46, 47, 48, 49, 50, and 51. Ask the teams to read their Scriptures and the material about them in the "Enter the Bible Story." Have them discuss the following questions: What challenges you or makes you curious about the Scripture passage? What does it say to you about God? What feelings or thoughts do you have about the way God is portrayed in the Scripture? What, if any, hope does the Scripture passage offer?

Discuss News Events

Distribute several recent copies of newspapers to the group and invite them to locate stories about other nations. Ask: What do you think Jeremiah might say to address the events in these stories? How do you think God might be at work in these contemporary events?

Live the Story

Read aloud the material in "Live the Story." Ask: How can our congregation offer hope and renewal to others? What are we already doing? What else might we do? List ideas on a markerboard. Invite the group to choose an idea from the list that would work as a ministry in the church or in the community. Close with the following prayer: God of hope and renewal, empower us to do your will and your work. Help us to offer justice, mercy, and compassion to all who suffer. In Christ we pray. Amen.

7. The Fall and Restoration of Jerusalem
Jeremiah 26–45; 52

Faith Focus

We want to hear good things about ourselves without being called to accountability for our behaviors. Christians are called to examine our hearts for places where we may need to change.

Before the Session

Pray for God's guidance during your time of preparation, and pray for the participants in your Immersion Bible study group. Read the Scriptures for Session 7 and jot down any questions or insights that emerge for you. Consider what questions might emerge from your group. Read Chapter 7. Before the participants arrive, write the Faith Focus on a markerboard or a large sheet of paper for all to see.

Claim Your Story

Read or review highlights of "Claim Your Story." Invite participants to tell about times in their lives when they or someone they know has refused to accept responsibility for their behaviors. Ask: What was the situation? What was the result? What could have been done differently?

Enter the Bible Story
Discuss Good News and Bad News

Have the participants form three teams. Assign a Scripture passage to each team as follows: Team One—Chapter 27, Team Two—Chapter 28, and Team Three—Chapter 29. Instruct the teams to read their assigned Scriptures and review highlights of the sections "Disputes Regarding God's Plan" and "Who's Right?" Tell them to discuss the following questions: What is the bad news in the Scripture? What good news, if any, do you see? What does the Scripture say to you about the human need to hear good news? about not wanting to hear bad news? What thoughts or feelings do you have about Jeremiah's insistence upon communicating bad news from God? Who would you identify as the prophets of bad news in our world? What do you think are the benefits and consequences of accepting the reality of bad news? How do you see God at work in reports of good news? in reports of bad news?

Explore Jeremiah's Understanding of a New Covenant

Invite a participant to read aloud Jeremiah 31:31-34. Review highlights of "The New Covenant" and the sidebar "Across the Testaments." Ask: What does it mean to you when Jeremiah says, "I will put my law within them, and I will write it on their hearts." What does it say to you about Jeremiah's understanding of

God's relationship to the people of Judah? What does this say to you about God's desire for relationships among humans and for relationship with God? What hope does it offer?

Reflect on Jeremiah's Suffering

Review highlights of Jeremiah 37 and 38 and the section "Dire Times." Ask: How do you respond to Jeremiah's determined pronouncements about the coming disaster for Judah even though it led to his imprisonment? How do his actions inspire you or challenge you?

Live the Story

Read aloud the Faith Focus and the section "Live the Story." Invite participants to consider times when "truth hurts." Ask: What positive opportunities emerge from hearing how we might need to make a change in our lives? Invite participants to pray silently about one change they can make for the better in their lives this week. Close with the following prayer: God of hope, thank you for your love and your forgiveness. Write your law on our hearts. Lead us to new life. In Christ we pray. Amen.

8. Mourning for Jerusalem's Holocaust
Lamentations

Faith Focus

We know through personal experience or through the lives of those close to us what it is like to face an apparently overwhelming tragedy. Christians find comfort in remembering that God loves us and is with us in the midst of any suffering and that God is working to bring us back into the fullness of life.

Before the Session

Pray for God's guidance during your time of preparation, and pray for the participants in your Immersion Bible study group. Read the Scriptures for Session 8 and jot down any questions or insights that emerge for you. Consider what questions might emerge from your group. Read Chapter 8. Before the participants arrive, write the Faith Focus on a markerboard or a large sheet of paper for all to see. Gather newspapers or news magazine stories of great communal disasters such as floods, earthquakes, or civil war.

Claim Your Story

Read the Faith Focus aloud. Read aloud the material in "Claim the Story." Invite participants to respond to the following questions from this section: What do you do when your world falls apart? How do you endure? What helps your faith survive?

Enter the Bible Story

Prepare Reports

Have the group form five teams. Assign a chapter of Lamentations to each of the teams. Ask them to read their assigned chapter and any material about it in the study book. Have them discuss the following questions: What is the primary theme for the lament in this chapter? What images or ideas stand out for you? Why? What disturbs you? Why? What does the chapter say to you about the poet's view of God? about the poet's view of the people? What hope, if any do you see in the chapter? Have each of the teams choose someone to report to the entire group about the contents of the chapter and the highlights of their discussion.

Share News Reports

Have participants return to their original five teams. Read aloud the sidebar "About the Christian Faith." Ask: How do you respond to the comments of Richard Nelson? Give newspaper or news magazine stories to each team. Tell them to identify similarities and differences between the news stories and the laments they explored in the chapters from Lamentations. Ask: How do you think God is present and active in the contemporary tragedy? How do you think we demonstrate God's power and care in the midst of tragedy? Invite the teams to share highlights of their discussions with the entire group.

Discuss "Remember, O Lord"

Review highlights of "Remember O Lord" and the sidebar "Across the Testaments." Ask: How do the examples of God remembering the covenant people offer hope? How does our remembering what God has already done and what God continues to do offer hope? In what ways, if any, does remembering God's presence and support change our feelings during tragedy?

Live the Story

Read aloud the Faith Focus and the section "Live the Story." Give each participant paper and pen or markers. Invite them to reflect silently on the time of tragedy or loss in their own life or in the life of someone they know. Invite them to write a prayer lament addressed to God or to create a drawing that expresses their mourning. Reassure them that they will not be obligated to share their lament with the group; however, if anyone feels a need to share their lament with the group, allow time to do so. Close with the following prayer: God of hope and restoration, we offer you our pain. We pray for your guidance as we seek ways to support one another during times of tragedy. In Christ we pray. Amen.

IMMERSE YOURSELF IN ANOTHER VOLUME

IMMERSION
Bible Studies

Available at Cokesbury and other booksellers   **AbingdonPress.com**